VITA[MIN]

"It is now *known* [that] today in the Western world can be helped by the correct dosage of 'micronutrients'—the minerals and vitamins that should be present in our bodies in ideal levels, but that we have allowed to get out of balance with appalling results. . . . VITAMIN VITALITY is an excellent handbook to the whole subject of vitamins and minerals for health and well-being, both mental and physical. Its information is accurate and its warnings only too timely. Good nutritional therapy is the only true preventative medicine. It is the medicine of the future— we have already waited too long."

—Carl C. Pfeiffer, M.D., Ph.D.
from the Foreword to *Vitamin Vitality*

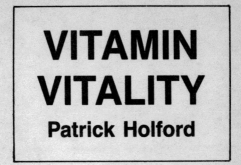

VITAMIN VITALITY

Patrick Holford

Foreword by
Carl C. Pfeiffer, M.D., Ph.D.

BANTAM BOOKS
TORONTO · NEW YORK · LONDON · SYDNEY · AUCKLAND

VITAMIN VITALITY
A Bantam Book

PRINTING HISTORY
First published in Great Britain in 1985
Bantam edition / November 1986

Illustrations by Dave Eaton.

ISBN 0-553-26230-0

Bantam Books are published by Bantam Books, Inc. Its trade-
mark, consisting of the words "Bantam Books" and the por-
trayal of a rooster, is Registered in U.S. Patent and Trademark
Office and in other countries. Marca Registrada. Bantam
Books, Inc., 666 Fifth Avenue, New York, New York 10103.

PRINTED IN THE UNITED STATES OF AMERICA

O   0 9 8 7 6 5 4 3 2 1

Acknowledgments

For their kind permission to reproduce material from published works I am grateful to: Bantam Books, Inc., for the diet and nutrient diagrams on p. 101 from Roger J. Williams, *The Wonderful World Within You*, 1977; Thorsons Publishers, Ltd., for the "Heart Check" on p. 94 from Patrick Holford, *The Whole Health Manual*, 1983; John Wiley & Sons, Ltd., for research from Rutter and Jones, *Lead versus Health*, 1983.

There is always someone behind the scenes "without whom this book couldn't have been written." This book is no exception. My thanks go to Professor John Dickerson, Professor Derek Bryce-Smith, and Dr. Carl Pfeiffer, for their invaluable research and for their care in checking parts of this book; also to Dr. Michael Colgan, Dr. Roy Walford, Dr. Stephen Davies, Dr. Roger Williams, and Dr. Donald Dickenson, whose thorough work has saved me hours of time hunting for the relevant references. My special thanks go to Tony Searby, Laura Swaffield, Betty Styles, my publishers Collins, and, most of all, to Liz Holford for providing me with inspiration.

Chapter 10 was written by **Liz Holford**
Chapter 11 was written by **Tony Searby**

Guide to Abbreviated Measures

1 gram (g) = 1,000 milligrams (mg) =
1,000,000 micrograms (mcg)

Most vitamins are measured in milligrams or micrograms. Vitamins A, D, and E are also measured in International Units (IU), a measurement designed to provide standardization of the different forms of these vitamins that have different potencies.

$$1\text{mcg of retinol } or \text{ 2mcg of beta carotene } =$$
$$3.3 \text{ IU of vitamin A}$$
$$40\text{mcg of vitamin D} = 1 \text{ IU}$$
$$1\text{mg of vitamin E} = 1 \text{ IU of alpha tocopherol}$$

For research purposes, measurements of minerals in the blood are expressed in micrograms per deciliter (mcg/dl); those in the hair in part per million (ppm).

Foreword

Complacent physicians claim all too often that certain diseases are, so to speak, "acts of God": that their cause is unknown and their cure uncertain. But over the last twenty years or so our knowledge of the essential role that vitamins and minerals play in health care has been increasing at a phenomenal rate. It is a role crucial not only in preserving and maintaining health, but also in restoring it to diseased patients. It is now *known* that many diseases common today in the western world can be helped by the correct dosage of "micronutrients"—the minerals and vitamins that should be present in our bodies in ideal levels, but that we have allowed to get out of balance with appalling results.

Two of the commonest findings in patients at my clinic over the years have been excessive levels of copper, caused by the water supply, and deficiency of nutrients such as zinc and manganese, caused by a diet of junk food. Many people develop crippling allergies unknown to previous generations, purely through their involuntary exposure to pollutants in the air they breathe and the food they eat. But it is my firmly held belief that with an adequate daily intake of micronutrients—essential substances that we *need* to nourish us—most chronic diseases would simply not exist.

Vitamin Vitality is an excellent handbook to the whole subject of vitamins and minerals for health and well-being, both mental and physical. Its information is accurate and its warnings only too timely. Good nutritional therapy is the only true preventative medicine. It is the medicine of the future—we have already waited too long for it.

Carl C. Pfeiffer, M.D., Ph.D.
Doctor and Psychiatrist
Princeton
New Jersey

Introduction

Today we are on the edge of the birth of a new form of health care, based not on intervention, but on cooperation with nature. It is all too easy to be blinded by science—organ transplants, microsurgery, new drug discoveries. But have these really helped to improve our health and the quality of our lives? This century we have witnessed control of infectious diseases that has saved the lives of many children, but we have also seen a vast increase in cancer, heart disease, and even arthritis. In fact, for all our technology, a man aged 45 today can only expect to live for two more years than the same man in 1920: until he is 74, as opposed to 72. And what of the quality of life? More than 124 million prescriptions are written every year in the USA for antidepressants, hypnotics, and tranquilizers, which hardly reflects a happy and healthy society.

The human body consists of about 30 trillion cells, most of which are repaired and replaced every year, and a mind so fine that it would take a computer the size of California to mimic its ability—if there was anyone to program it. The cells of the human body are essentially very similar to the cells of other animals: it is clear that we have evolved our intricacy and perfection over millions of years. While you read this book your body is digesting foods, breathing air, repairing cells, and keeping the blood flowing to every one of your organs. Isn't it rather arrogant to assume that we can simply whip out one organ and replace it with a new one, or swallow a drug when the body chemistry has lost its natural balance? Shouldn't we rather be asking *why* the organ doesn't work, or *why* the body chemistry is unbalanced?

By trying to keep healthy in the first place we can reduce our dependence on surgery and debilitating drugs—perhaps even dispense with them altogether. No animal can adapt to markedly changed conditions in as short a time as two hundred years and there is no reason to assume that we have successfully adapted to breathe polluted air, drink polluted water, and eat foods containing additives. By improving our environment, including our food, there is good reason to believe that we can attain a level of health free from disease, characterized by well-being, mental alertness, and physical energy as well as an extended life span.

However, we don't have to live like cavemen to avoid the ravages of the twentieth century. Indeed, for cavemen— just as for most wild animals today—suboptimum nutrition was the rule. Animals compete for their food. Many species become extinct, and those that are stronger or more suited to their environment survive. But take those animals out of their natural environment and give them optimum levels of vitamins and minerals and interesting things happen. Tests have shown that the life span of fish can be tripled, dogs can grow larger and live longer, and all animals show signs of increased health.

The same is true for us. With optimum nutrition we too can move toward optimum health. But, you might ask, aren't we optimally nourished already? The answer is no. Much like the animals, suboptimum nutrition is still the rule for us too. To help prevent obvious malnutrition, most countries have set Recommended Daily Allowances (RDAs) for vitamins, and also add certain vitamins to common foods. Yet we don't as a rule get even these basic levels in the so-called "well-balanced" diet. And Recommended Daily Allowances *are* basic; they should not be confused with the vitamin requirements needed for *optimum* health, which may be as much as twenty times greater.

The following chapters set out to show how intelligence and memory may be increased, physical energy improved, and diseases prevented, all by altering the vitamins and minerals in our diet. But nutrition is not the only factor involved. Our level of exercise, degree of exposure to pollution, and the stresses and strains imposed by our life-style all affect our health as well as our nutritional needs. All these factors and more must be taken into account in order to work out our individual vitamin and mineral needs. In this book I explain the principles involved, helping each of you to work out your own personal health program.

We now have the knowledge and the resources to create a civilization more free of disease than ever before. If you follow the principles outlined in this book, I believe you will experience a level of health and vitality beyond your greatest expectations.

Wishing you more than good health,

1

The Vitamin Controversy

We need to eat at least 45 different substances to keep
ourselves in good health, including carbohydrates, fats,
proteins, minerals, and vitamins. Although vitamins are
supplied in tiny amounts compared to protein, for example, they are no less important. For instance, our daily
requirement for vitamin B_{12} is considerably less than a
millionth of our protein requirement. But without this
0.000005g of B_{12} we cannot live, since it helps make the
red blood cells that carry oxygen to every part of our
bodies.

By definition, vitamins are substances that have to be
supplied in our diet. Without them we cannot maintain
normal health, adequate growth, and, in most cases, life
itself. Although some substances, such as vitamin D, do
not entirely fit this description (vitamin D can be made in
the skin with adequate sunlight), I cover in this book all
nutrients the amounts of which supplied by the diet affect
our health and vitality. They include vitamin B_1 (thiamine), B_2 (riboflavin), B_3 (niacin or niacinamide), B_5
(pantothenic acid), B_6 (pyridoxine), B_{12} (cyanocobalamine),
folic acid, biotin, PABA (para-amino-benzoic acid), inositol, and choline—together, all these are called the B
Complex vitamins; vitamin C (ascorbic acid); the bioflavanoids
(rutin, hesperidin, citrus bioflavanoids)—known as the C
Complex; and finally vitamins A (retinol or beta-carotene),
D (ergocalciferol and cholecalciferol), E (tocopherol), and
K—these last four must be supplied together with dietary
fat to be absorbed as they are "fat-soluble". This means
that they are stored more readily in the body than those
that are "water-soluble", which do not store and are
needed much more on a daily basis.

Since all vitamins (except B_{12}) are made by plants or microorganisms in the soil, we need to eat fruits and vegetables including grains, beans, pulses, nuts, and seeds to get them. Alternatively, we can eat meat or fish, which has, in turn, gathered vitamins from the vegetable kingdom. Meat and fish tend to be good sources of the fat-soluble vitamins since they are stored in the animal, while fruits and vegetables are our best sources of the B vitamins and vitamin C.

While protein, fats, and carbohydrates can be seen as our basic fuel—"the stuff we're made of"—vitamins are the nuts and bolts, the catalysts and regulators that keep everything running smoothly. Not one of your 30 trillion cells can be made without vitamins—they are vital for energy, the nerves, mental and emotional balance, skin, hair and all the senses. They may protect us from all major diseases, including cancer, heart disease, and arthritis, and strengthen us against colds and other infections. Table 1 gives the basic functions and the best sources of these vitamins.

However, recent research has found out that it's not so much the type of food we eat, but what has been done to the food that is important. For instance, an orange grown in mineral-poor soil produces less than half as much vitamin C as one grown in good soil. Store the orange for two weeks and it has only half as much vitamin C again. Cooking, refining, and other forms of food processing further reduce the vitamin content, often by as much as half. Boil a vegetable for 20 minutes and 40 percent of the B and C vitamins are destroyed. Refine brown flour to make white and 78 percent of the zinc, chromium, and manganese are lost.

So, to protect us from the dangers of vitamin deficiency, the governments of most countries have set Recommended Daily Allowances (RDAs) for some nutrients, albeit only for six out of the 16 nutrients. These RDAs are "estimated to exceed the requirements of most individuals and thereby to ensure that the needs of nearly all the population are met."[1] But if this really was the case why are $1.77 billion spent every year on supplements? Nearly half of the

Vitamin	Why it is necessary	Best sources in food
A	Needed for healthy skin, resistance to infection, and good eyesight, particularly in the dark.	Fish liver, eggs, dairy, produce, carrots, beets, and green leafy vegetables.
B Complex	Vital for energy, nervous balance, emotional balance, hair, skin, and nails.	Raw vegetables, nuts, wholegrains, seeds, beans, lentils, yeast, eggs, and milk produce.
C	Protects against infection and many poisons; helps maintain skin, bones, and cartilage and helps to heal wounds.	Raw fruits, fruit juices, peppers, berries, tropical fruits.
D	Helps maintain calcium balance in bones and teeth, helps to prevent tooth decay and brittle bones.	Fish, milk, egg yolk; also made in the presence of sunlight.
E	Helps maintain muscles, especially the heart; prevents blood clots; helps to heal wounds.	Vegetable oils, nuts, seeds, wheatgerm.
K	Helps blood to clot. Extra is required only in conditions in which the blood does not clot.	Spinach, cabbage, cauliflower.

Table 1

American population take supplements regularly throughout the year. Are they being conned or is our diet not as good as it should be?

It isn't just our diet that's at fault but also our understanding of RDAs. Despite the fact that even the National Research Council admits they're not enough for everybody, most people assume they are. Also, vital nutrients like manganese, chromium, and selenium are often considered inessential just because no RDAs exist for them.

The National Research Council admits that children, the elderly, or those who are pregnant are especially at risk. And that "special needs for nutrients arising from such problems as premature birth, inherited metabolic disorders, infections, chronic diseases, and the use of medications require special dietary and therapeutic measures." With 31 million people suffering from chronic diseases,[2] 25 million elderly people, one in ten people having inherited metabolic deficiencies that cause them to need more of some nutrients, 3.3 million new mothers,[3] and more than half the population on medication that interferes with the action of micronutrients, good grounds could be made for most of the population needing more than the RDAs.

Having said this, does the average American diet even supply these often inadequate levels? According to government surveys the answer is an equivocal no. The USDA Household Food Consumption Survey in 1977–78 revealed that "half of the households had diets that failed to meet the allowances (RDAs) for one or more nutrients."[4] A fifth of diets surveyed provided less than two-thirds of the RDA for calcium, vitamin A, or vitamin C. In the Ten-State Nutrition Survey "a significant proportion of the population surveyed was found to be malnourished or was at high risk of developing nutritional problems."[5]

More than a hundred independent surveys have come to the same conclusion that nutritional deficiency is epidemic. One showed that New York children were low in blood levels of B_1, B_2, folic acid, iron, and zinc. Another found iron and folic acid deficient in 30 percent of people tested in Miami.[6]

To understand the confusion and contradiction surrounding vitamins, it is essential to take a closer look both at the figures and at the points of view of some of the organizations that produce the statistics.

The Department of Health and Social Security (DHSS) and the Ministry of Agriculture, Food and Fisheries (MAFF) are the two official bodies in the UK responsible for nutritional policymaking. MAFF describes proteins as "body-building"; carbohydrates as "energy-giving" and vitamins as "protective"—that is, they protect us against known vitamin-deficiency diseases such as scurvy.[7] This misconceived and oversimplified view gives rise to popular slogans such as "eat steaks for muscle" or "sugar for energy". These slogans are misleading.

Eating extra protein, or taking protein powders, can only build a fraction more muscle even in the most dedicated body-builder. With hard training, the maximum amount of muscle that can be built in a year will be less than 8lb. That represents a gain of 2½oz each week, or ⅓oz a day. And only 22 percent of muscle is protein. So an increased protein consumption of less than ⅒oz a day—about a quarter of a teaspoonful!—is all that is needed to bring about the greatest possible muscle gain. Yet body-builders often think that the more steaks they can eat, the more muscle they will be able to build!

The same mistaken ideas exist about sugar. The average sugar consumption per person per year is 128lb[8]—equivalent to almost a quarter of our entire calorie requirement. Little room is left for foods that are nutritious. The vast majority of us eat far more calories than we need; the consumption of extra sugar is not going to give us any more energy. Our immediate "reserve tank" of energy is the glycogen that is stored in our liver and muscle cells; in most of us this is kept constantly full. Yet athletes insist on taking glucose or dextrose, simple forms of sugar that can be converted into glycogen. Marathon runners "stack up" before a race by eating plates of spaghetti for the same reason—carbohydrate is a complex sugar. Yet I believe that a balanced meal the evening before a race is enough to maximize the glycogen store. Extra sugar doesn't help—it hinders.

There are circumstances in which the glycogen store is used up—notably in crash dieting. With the loss of glycogen, the body loses considerable amounts of water—together, these can cause body weight to decrease by as much as 5lb in one week. But it isn't fat that's lost, just water and glycogen. Three days of normal calorie intake will restore the glycogen—and, of course, the weight. So much for crash diets.

Recommended Daily Allowances and Average Daily Intake for an 18–34-year-old (moderately active)

Nutrient	RDA	Average Daily Intake	Average Daily Intake as a %age of RDA
Vitamin A	4,000 IU	4,480 IU	120%
Vitamin B_1 (Thiamine)	1mg	1.15mg	115%
Vitamin B_2 (Riboflavin)	1.2mg	1.87mg	156%
Vitamin B_3	13mg	29.1mg	224%
Vitamin C	60mg	59.1mg	98%
Calcium	800mg	950mg	118%
Iron	18mg	10.9mg	60%

Table 2

The idea of the human body as a machine that needs fuel gives rise to the belief that if you give it more fuel, it will run for longer. But it is not more fuel we need—it is more efficiency, more miles to the gallon. And the key to efficiency is the intake of vitamins and minerals, because these are involved in more than 90 percent of the chemical reactions that occur in our bodies. Their role is so fundamental that even the slightest deficiency threatens our health and performance.

The Recommended Daily Allowances (RDAs) for nutrients are established by the National Research Council to protect us from the obvious vitamin-deficiency diseases. Table 2 sets out the levels for the main nutrients. The nutrient content of food is calculated from standard tables and no comment is made about the enormous variation of nutrient content known to exist in foods. For example, we know that vitamin C in fruit varies enormously. The assumption is that over a year one would find that an average of 66mg would be provided per orange. But vitamin C is needed every day: what use is an "average" intake for the year when the variation from week to week could easily make most of us deficient? Twice as much vitamin C one day will not make up for a deficiency another day, since its storage in the body is minimal.

Furthermore, the averages arrived at tend to conceal another disturbing conclusion. Since each person taking in more than the RDA boosts the total "average" intake, it follows that someone else must be getting much less than is necessary. To be sure that *nobody* is deficient in a particular vitamin, its average consumption would need to be as high as 200 percent of the RDA. When this is taken into account, it is seen that perhaps approaching 50 percent of people are likely to be deficient in vitamin B_1, and a large number deficient in vitamin B_2 and iron.

The results themselves are of course not cooked, but the foods certainly are. Food processing and cooking inevitably lead to losses of some vitamins. This is taken into account in the figures for vitamins B_1 and C, but not for vitamins B_2 and B_3 and calcium. Soluble calcium in milk, for instance, becomes insoluble when the milk is heated,[9] while pasteurizing destroys the enzyme phosphatase, which aids the assimilation of calcium in the body.[10] Vegetables lose 30 to 40 percent of their vitamin B_2 and B_3 content when cooked.[11] Since this factor is not taken into account, it is almost certain that many people consume less absorbable B_2, B_3 and calcium than the recommended levels.

A more reliable indicator of vitamin intake than analysis of diet is "functional enzyme testing", which measures the chemical reactions in blood that depend on the presence of certain vitamins. If a vitamin is in short supply, the relevant reaction will be impaired. RDAs are calculated to include a large safety margin, so one would not expect these tests to reveal clinical deficiency except in rare cases. However, one study found that out of 431 students 11.1 percent were deficient in vitamin B_2.[12] Another study on geriatric hospital patients found that 44 percent showed a deficiency of B_1, B_2, or B_6.[13, 14] The elderly are particularly at risk from iron and folic acid deficiency. One survey found that 78 out of 93 geriatric patients had a deficiency of at least one of these B vitamins.[15]

Highest International Recommended Daily Allowances		
Nutrient	**USA RDA**	**Highest RDA**
Vitamin A	4,000 IU	5,000 IU (USSR)
Vitamin B$_1$ (Thiamine)	1mg	1.8mg (USSR)
Vitamin B$_2$ (Riboflavin)	1.2mg	2.4mg (USSR)
Vitamin B$_3$	13mg	18mg (UK)
Vitamin C	60mg	120mg (USSR)
Calcium	800mg	800mg (USA)
Iron	18mg	18mg (USA)

Table 3

Recommended Daily Allowances and Average Daily Intake for an 18–34-year-old (moderately active)			
Nutrient	**Highest International RDA**	**Average Daily Intake**	**Average Daily Intake as a percentage of RDA**
Vitamin A	5,000 IU	4,480 IU	89% (deficient)
Vitamin B$_1$ (Thiamine)	1.8mg	1.15mg	64% (deficient)
Vitamin B$_2$ (Riboflavin)	2.4mg	1.87mg	78% (deficient)
Vitamin B$_3$	18mg	29.1mg	162%
Vitamin C	120mg	59.1mg	49% (deficient)
Calcium	800mg	950mg	119% (borderline)
Iron	18mg	10.9mg	60% (deficient)

Table 4

The National Advisory Committee on Nutrition Education (NACNE), set up in 1973 and headed by Professor W. James, is not complacent about vitamin C either. Its report points out that "perhaps 10 percent of households have been estimated to consume less than 30mg of vitamin C per head" and "up to 14 percent of elderly groups surveyed when over 70 years of age have been found to have clear evidence of folic acid deficiency".[16]

And remember, when such statements talk about deficiency, they usually mean according to the RDAs, which are themselves only recommended levels, estimated by a rule of thumb. A comparison of the RDAs of the USA, UK, Australia, New Zealand, Canada, and West Germany shows considerable variation in the estimation of acceptable daily allowances.[17] Since it is our health at stake, wouldn't it be better to take the highest, and therefore safest, estimated RDAs? These are shown in Table 3.

Table 4 compares these RDAs with the USA average diet. We now find that deficiencies in almost every nutrient are likely to occur in at least half of the population. Clearly the solution lies in legislation and campaigning to improve the American diet. But the National Academy of Sciences sees another solution: lower the RDAs! New proposed RDAs, the first since 1980, were due to be released in 1985. But the suggestions for lowering these already too low levels caused such an outcry among committee members that no changes have been made.

The Myth of the Average Orange

To produce these official figures, diets are "analyzed" by adding up the weight of the foods eaten and calculating the quantities of nutrients in them using standard tables. But just how accurate are these tables? The "average American orange" contains 66mg of vitamin C. Nutritionist Dr. Michael Colgan, of San Diego, California, decided to test these figures for himself. First he tested some oranges from a supermarket. They looked, smelled, and tasted perfectly normal, but contained less than 1mg of vitamin C. Probably they had been stored for a long time. Then he analyzed an orange picked that day: it contained 180mg.[18] The average may indeed have been about 66mg, but what use in practice is an average figure if the variation around it is so wide? Similarly large differences in vitamin content have been found by the American Medical Association and the US Department of Agriculture. [19, 20] Table 5 shows some of them.

And, unfortunately, the bad news doesn't end there. RDAs in the UK are calculated only for vitamins A, D, C, B_1, B_2, B_3, iron, and calcium. The National Research

Variations in nutrient content in common foods (per 100g of food)		
Vitamin A	in carrots	70 to 18,500 IU
Vitamin B$_5$	in whole wheat flour	0.3 to 3.3mg
Vitamin C	in oranges	0 to 116mg
Vitamin E	in wheat germ	3.2 to 21 IU
Iron	in spinach	0.1 to 158mg
Manganese	in lettuce	0.1 to 16.9mg

Table 5

Council for the USA also makes recommendations for daily intakes of vitamins B$_6$, B$_{12}$, folic acid, vitamin E, magnesium, zinc, phosphorus, and iodine. All these nutrients still represent only 16 out of the 26 vitamins and minerals known to be essential for normal life processes.

While no RDAs exist in Britain for 18 of these nutrients, they are no less important constituents of a well-balanced diet. A research paper in 1979 pointed out the low or borderline levels of magnesium, copper, zinc, vitamin B$_6$, and folic acid in the British diet.[21] Other surveys have added the minerals selenium and chromium to this list.

In 1979 the DHSS recommended a daily intake of 300mcg of the B vitamin, folic acid, which was considerably below the USA recommendation of 400mcg. However, in 1981 this recommendation was withdrawn—perhaps because the average British diet appeared to contain nowhere near this level.[22] Now, when we have proof that spina bifida in babies can be prevented if mothers have high levels of folic acid in their diet,[23] we may wonder if we are being lulled into a false sense of security.

Selenium, a mineral vital for preventing heart disease and cancer,[24] is now included in almost every animal feed in the USA and Canada. The estimated savings per year from the prevention of disease and loss of animals is over $100 million. The Food and Drug Administration recommends a daily intake for people of 50 to 200mcg to maintain general well-being; it is unlikely that as many as ten percent of the British population get this much.

George Briggs, a prominent professor of nutrition at the University of California at Berkeley said: "The typical diet is a national disaster. If I fed it to pigs or cows, without adding vitamins and other supplements, I could wipe out the entire livestock industry."[25]

Health Doesn't Equal Wealth

For any government, proof of inadequate diet in the population can be a public embarrassment and a financial nightmare. If our diet provides only half of the folic acid that we need, what should be done? Free supplements for all are expensive. Antibiotics are known to destroy the beneficial intestinal bacteria involved in the production and absorption of B vitamins, yet vitamin B supplements are not given with antibiotic treatment.

Perhaps a more fruitful area in which to work for improvement is the food industry. Tighter legislation could reduce the degree to which food is "denutrientized" before it is sold. The profits for major food manufacturers lie in their ability to refine foods so that they can be kept for a long time; the white flour used in most commercially made loaves has so few nutrients left in it that not even a weevil could live on it! One vegetable oil company removes vitamin E (naturally present in all seeds to provide protection against rancidity) in the refining process, and then sells it to the vitamin industry. The oil, deficient in vitamin E, is then sold to the public, who may—or may not—choose to spend more money in buying separate supplements of vitamin E! But tighter legislation concerning the removal of nutrients, or encouraging the addition of nutrients, would be very bad news for most major food manufacturers. Professor Bryce-Smith, renowned for his work in exposing the dangers of lead, has been quick to point out that the most dangerous mineral to man is not lead—it's gold!

The food manufacturers themselves apply pressure through independent associations and societies that are involved with our health and good nutrition. "Just fifty organizations control most of the nation's food industries and

products, and they have gone to great lengths to promote
the image that factory processing is merely an extension of
of family cooking," says Dr. Ray Walford.[26]

Most food manufacturers would openly admit that their
primary reason for being in business is to make money, not
to promote or demote the nation's health. In the end, it is
up to us, the public, to *demand* foods with their full
complement of vitamins and minerals, and foods without
salt, sugar, or refined flours. As the demand increases,
more and more companies will have to sell healthier
produce. For the time being, however, it is very difficult
to maintain optimum health and nutrition without taking
supplements.

Supplementary Benefit

With the growing demand for healthy food and for vitamins, the money now spent on supplements exceeds $1.77
billion each year in the USA, which is still only a fraction
of the money spent each year on drugs. But with an 11
percent growth of the vitamin market each year have come
tighter controls on quality and advertising. But it is far
from clear whether these laws are designed to protect the
consumer or to promote the sales of the pharmaceutical
industries. Drugs can be patented, and the drug company
then has a monopoly on sales for a number of years.
Vitamins, being natural constituents of foods, cannot be
patented. Consequently, few companies invest money in
nutrition research since their competitors would benefit
equally from their investment.

But the pharmaceutical industry does, on the other
hand, have a vested interest in banning or restricting the
sale of vitamin and mineral supplements over the counter
in health food shops; in this way it stands to gain more
sales, more profits, and a tighter control over who is
allowed to sell vitamins. At the time of writing, pressure is
being put on the National Research Council to lower the
RDAs. In Britain, a paper proposing serious restrictions
on the sale of nutrients without an RDA is once again
being prepared for presentation to Parliament. In Canada

a new form of dietary fiber, which helps diabetics reduce their need for insulin, has been withdrawn from sale in health food shops on the grounds that it is "medicinal" and should therefore be obtainable only on prescription. In Australia selenium, a mineral crucial in protection against cancer, is similarly restricted on the grounds that extremely large doses could be dangerous—but other countries do not ban it. It seems that every year the health food and vitamin companies have to fight harder for the right to sell better health to the nation.

2

Each Person's Needs Are Unique

Even if our diet meets all the Recommended Daily Allowances, it is almost impossible to get all our *optimum* nutrient requirements from diet alone. I say almost, because out of at least 1,000 clients of mine, only five have shown no suboptimum signs of vitamin deficiency. However, diet is of course crucial for providing the basic levels of most nutrients and obviously for supplying adequate quantities of carbohydrates (including fiber), fats, and protein.

The difference between obtaining the basic nutrient requirements and the optimum nutrient requirements is the difference between moderate health and excellent health. By obtaining optimum levels of each nutrient for a minimum of six months, our bodies are able to replace old cells with healthy new cells. Within one year most of our cells will be replaced as new. Just think—a new you every 12 months!

The levels of nutrients you need as an individual to provide optimum nutritional support are dependent on a wealth of factors, some of them seemingly unconnected with nutrition. To arrive at the most suitable nutritional program for you, all these must be carefully evaluated. The eight major factors vital for good health are shown in Figure 1 and described below.

Heredity: Have You Got Good Parents?

Optimum nutrition is different for every one of us: no two people ever have the same vitamin requirements, just as no two people ever look the same. Our nutrient needs, like our looks, are partly dependent on our parents and grandparents. Small nutrient deficiencies in our ancestors

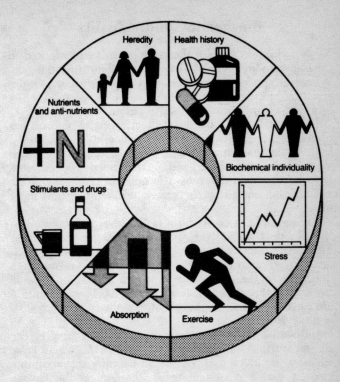

Figure 1 Factors that affect nutritional needs

may cause increased nutrient needs in us. A recent study by Lucille Hurley at the University of California induced a short-term zinc deficiency into a group of pregnant rats. Their offspring showed weakened immune systems—a condition associated with zinc deficiency—despite having adequate zinc status all their lives. Their offspring in turn *also* had poor immune function and so did the next generation— all because of a transient zinc deficiency three generations earlier![1]

Biochemical Individuality

No two children born of the same parents and exposed to the same environment will have identical nutritional needs. Whatever the circumstances, every individual is unique, and this biochemical uniqueness must be assessed when building an optimum nutrition program.

Professor Roger Williams of the University of Texas has established the scientific fact of biochemical individuality, both for animals and humans.[2] Vast differences in organ size, enzyme production, and nutrient needs are commonly found. Ten-fold differences in nutrient requirement are not uncommon, although three-fold differences are more usual.

For example, a comparison of the level of vitamin A in the blood of 92 individuals found a 30-fold difference.[3] This result suggests a wide range among people in their need for vitamin A. One of the early signs of vitamin A deficiency is the occurrence of mouth ulcers: for some of my clients these occur if less than 20,000 IU of vitamin A are consumed each day, but for others, the RDA of 2,500 IU is quite sufficient.

Individual variation in vitamin C needs is far greater.[4] By measuring the excretion of vitamin C when large amounts are given it is possible to measure the maximum amount that a person absorbs. Research at the Colgan Institute of Nutritional Science in San Diego, California, found that while seven percent of people reached their tissue saturation level with 500mg a day, five percent were still absorbing vitamin C at levels beyond 5,000mg a day.[5] Nobel prize winner Dr. Linus Pauling takes up to 10,000mg a day—a very far cry from the USA RDA of 60 mg.

Although vitamin B_6 has no RDA, a level of 2mg is thought to be sufficient—except in cases of premenstrual tension.[6, 7] Doses of 80 to 200mg of the vitamin have repeatedly been proved to help 70 percent of sufferers from PMT—a clear case for biochemical individuality.

These examples highlight the importance of the individual approach in finding out your own nutritional needs.

The orthodox method of dietary analysis—in which nutrients are calculated from standard food tables and compared to standard recommended daily levels—is nothing short of shooting in the dark.

Our health today is the result of our nutrition from the day we were conceived. Over the years, any deficiencies in our diet accumulate and symptoms of deficiency become more pronounced. These symptoms can be small, like lack of energy, poor skin, and poor memory; or severe, like arthritis, chronic depression, or heart disease. Often these symptoms become most apparent when we are under extra nutritional stress—for example, at puberty, during and after pregnancy, and during the menopause.

Vitamins, unlike drugs, tend to be slow to take effect. While most people experience an increase in energy within six weeks, improvement in memory, cardiovascular health, and resistance to infection rarely occur before three months have elapsed. As time goes on, health improves as more and more defective cells are replaced with healthy cells. While my health improved considerably when I started my own personal health program, some symptoms—like sensitivity to light—remained. Only after five years was I able to tolerate bright sunlight without wearing sunglasses or a hat.

Nutrients and Antinutrients

While you can change your diet to exclude refined and processed foods, some nutritional needs cannot be met even by dietary intervention. Mineral deficiencies vary from country to country, depending on a host of geological factors. Many countries in the northern hemisphere, including many parts of the United States, are low in selenium,[8] zinc, and manganese. This may be due to glaciation in the past, and overfarming in the present. Even the best organically-grown vegetables can only be as good as the soil they're grown in.

Often ignored in nutrition is the role of antinutrients—substances that interfere with the action of nutrients by preventing their absorption, disturbing their chemical utilization, or promoting their excretion from the body. Toxic metals like lead and copper are good examples of anti-nutrients; they interfere with zinc and calcium utilization.[9] Many natural foods contain small amounts of antinutrients. For example, wheat contains phytate which interferes with zinc absorption; an excessive consumption of wholemeal bread can, as a result, seriously deplete zinc levels. Phytates are also high in wheat bran, so a diet high in refined foods, with added bran to compensate, can actually do more harm than good. It is far better to obtain fiber from vegetables and wholegrains than from bran.

Since 1950 some 2,000 chemical additives have been put into popular foods, many of which act as antinutrients. Some of these are not easily excreted from the body, so intake of these and other antinutrients in the past must be taken into account as well as current intake. For example, the powerful insecticide DDT, although outlawed, was found in 119 out of 132 samples of mushrooms, apples, and lettuce analyzed in 1982. Once taken in, DDT can remain in the body for up to 50 years.

Absorption

For some nutrients such as the mineral manganese, as little as 0.5 percent of the amount supplied from the diet is absorbed.[10] Iron supplied from beef is 95 percent usable, but iron from an egg is only ten percent usable—unless the egg is eaten with orange juice, since vitamin C can quadruple the absorption of iron.[11] These examples illustrate the importance of the question of absorption. The most common reasons for poor absorption are:

Lack of enzymes to complete digestion (dependent on B vitamins)

Lack of hydrochloric acid in the stomach (dependent on B vitamins)

Excess of binding agents such as phytates

Poor intestinal bacteria needed to make some B vitamins

Competition between minerals at the absorption site (e.g. iron versus copper)

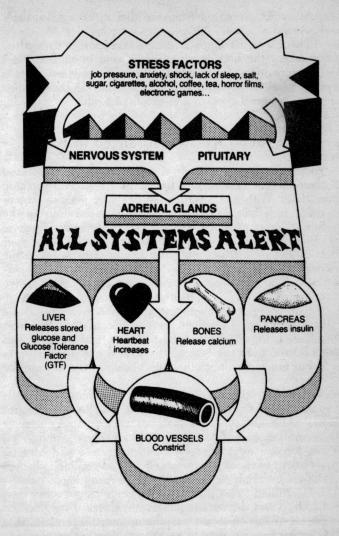

Figure 2 The stress reaction

Minerals presented from the diet in an unabsorbable
   form

The idea that spinach increases Popeye's strength is
mistaken: the high levels of oxalic acid in spinach block
the absorption of iron into the body! Even if your diet is
very good, your power of absorption may be the deciding
factor between average and excellent health.

Stress: Are You Addicted to It?

Suddenly, the car in front of you is much too close. You
slam on your brakes, with the car skidding. Will you stop
in time? With just a yard or so to spare, your car comes
safely to a halt. "I'd better drive more carefully in the
future!" you think to yourself as you breathe a sigh of
relief. For you, it seems, the worst is over. But for your
body the effects have only just begun. This is called the
stress reaction.

In 1956 a Canadian biochemist called Hans Selye
discovered a series of events that took place when an
animal was put into a threatening situation.[12] The pulse
rate went up, the blood vessels constricted, the liver
released sugar into the bloodstream and calcium was
mobilized from the bones. The animal was gearing up to
get as much glucose to the muscle cells as fast as possible.
Why?

In nature, there are two possible reactions to a threatening event: fight or flight. For man, the chemistry continues although we've learned not to fight and, in most
circumstances, not to run. Unlike the animal, we have no
use for that extra energy-producing glucose and have no
means to burn up the metabolites of adrenaline, which is
the chemical messenger that gets us ready for action.

Continued stress puts great demands on our nutritional
needs,[13] and disrupts our body chemistry if we have no
means to "let off steam". Optimum nutrition and suitable
exercise become doubly important. The major nutrients
used in the stress reaction are vitamins B_3, B_5 (pantothenic

acid), and C, and the minerals zinc, chromium, calcium, and manganese.

While living with stress would appear to be counter-productive, it is clear that many of us like the challenges and pressures of a stressful life. Our love of contact sports and dangerous activities such as fast driving or skiing strongly suggests that we are addicted to adrenaline. For animals, the most fearsome fighter is usually the best survivor. For man, this "killer" instinct, based on the love of the adrenaline reaction, is a potent reminder of our primal past.

Stimulants and Drugs

Stimulants like tea, coffee, sugar, cigarettes, and alcohol are best seen as nutritional stressors. Like fear, they also begin the stress reaction that is initiated by the release of adrenaline. Such stimulants can cause heart irregularities and excessive fluid loss, which lead to increased loss of minerals.[14] Like stress itself, they also rapidly use up levels of some vitamins and minerals without providing any replacement. For instance, every time we drink some coffee, chromium is released into the bloodstream to help stabilize blood sugar. When the process is over, the chromium is simply lost. Coffee provides us with no chromium to replace it. By the age of 30, most people's chromium stores are almost completely used up.[15] The diet of today provides less than 15 percent of the chromium estimated to have existed in the diet of our ancestors.[16]

Many common medical drugs interact with the vitamins and minerals in our bodies. Antibiotics deplete our store of the B Complex vitamins; the contraceptive pill depletes vitamin B_6 and zinc, thereby increasing copper absorption,[17] and many antacids contain toxic aluminium salts. The use of diuretic drugs also leads to significant losses of minerals, especially zinc.[18] Never could the adage "one man's meat, another man's poison" be more true than in relation to drugs. Drug researcher Professor Smith from St. Mary's Hospital in London has found that one person in ten has biochemical quirks that could cause them to react adversely to a whole range of supposedly "safe" medicines.[19] Normally, the bloodstream carries a drug directly from the intestines to the liver, where most of it is broken down by enzymes, leaving a small amount of the drug to get to work on the body itself. Whereas ten percent of a particular drug, for example, may finally be used by the average patient, some people, being unable to break it down, end up with 40 percent of the dose in their bodies, which can be lethal—another proof of biochemical individuality.

Exercise: Keeping on the Move

Other than age, exercise is the single most important factor to alter our overall nutritional requirements. An athlete in training may expend four times as many calories as a person leading a sedentary life-style. This creates a greatly increased demand for the vitamins and minerals involves in energy production. And lack of exercise causes a rapid loss of calcium—a problem encountered by astronauts during space flight programs because without gravity they couldn't get sufficient exercise to maintain normal calcium levels in the bones. Even a brisk walk three times a week can make a big difference to your calcium levels if you have a sedentary life-style.[20]

Health History

One of the factors that affect our personal condition is our health history. Every cold and broken bone can alter our nutritional needs, sometimes for many years to follow. For example, many women complain of symptoms and illnesses occurring after the birth of their first child. Why? Often the increased nutritional needs of pregnancy, which are not met by the average diet, are just enough to tip the scales towards the beginning of an illness. Coupled with the demands of beastfeeding and broken nights, many young mothers take years to recover their previous health and vitality. And vitamin and mineral needs change dramatically with any illness or accident. Optimum nutrition is doubly crucial at these times.

If you take all these factors into account, it is possible to increase and maintain a level of health far beyond average expectations—a level of health that is characterized not only by lack of illness, but by an abundance of energy and vitality and a positive sense of well-being. The following chapters show you how, with the proper use of diet and vitamins, you can increase your intelligence, energy, and performance, and extend your healthy life span by at least ten years.

3

Intelligence and Memory

When researcher Dr. Ruth Harrell heard of a case history reported by biochemist Mary Allen in which the IQ of a Down's syndrome child went from 20 to 90 points, she decided to explore the idea that many mentally retarded children might have been born with increased needs for certain vitamins and minerals. In her first study she took 22 mentally retarded children and divided them into two groups. One received supplements containing the vitamins and minerals listed in Table 6, the other received placebos (dummy tablets). After four months, the group taking the supplements had experienced an average increase in IQ of between five and 9.6 points; those on placebos showed no change. For the next four months, both groups of children were given the supplements and the average improvement was 10.2 points. Six of the Down's children had improvements of between ten and 25 IQ points![1]

The results seemed too good to be true. After all, Down's syndrome is a genetic disease, so how could vitamin supplements increase the intelligence of six of the children so dramatically? This sort of improvement in intelligence would put most of our educationally subnormal children back in normal classes!

These findings have since been confirmed by three studies—and contradicted by three more.[2] Why the apparent confusion? Researcher Dr. Alex Schauss may have found the answer: it appears that only those children taking thyroid treatment *and* supplements improved. Neither supplements nor thyroid treatment on their own are expected to help improve intelligence in Down's syndrome patients.

Nutrients used in Dr. Harrell's Study on Mental Retardation			
Vitamin A	15,000 IU	Vitamin C	1,500mg
Vitamin D	300 IU	Vitamin E	600 IU
Vitamin B_1	300mg	Magnesium	300mg
Vitamin B_2	200mg	Calcium	400mg
Vitamin B_3	750mg	Zinc	30mg
Vitamin B_5	490mg	Manganese	3mg
Vitamin B_6	350mg	Copper	1.75mg
Vitamin B_{12}	1,000mcg	Iron	7.5mg
Folic acid	400mcg	Iodine	0.15mg

Please note On no account should these levels be taken without professional guidance from a doctor or nutrition consultant

Table 6

Earlier work in nutrition, such as a study by Kubula in 1960,[3] had shown that increased vitamin status was associated with increased intelligence. He divided 351 students into high and low vitamin C groups, depending on the levels in their blood. The students' IQ was then measured and found to average 113 and 109 respectively: those with higher levels of vitamin C in their blood had an average of 4.5 IQ points more.

The fewer refined foods you eat the cleverer you are, concluded some researchers at the Massachusetts Institute for Technology. They found that the higher the proportion of refined carbohydrates—such as sugar, commercial cereals, white bread, and sweets—in the diet, the lower the IQ score. The difference was almost 25 points![4]

Great improvement in intelligence has also been shown with autistic children,[5] and those with learning difficulties. In a recent study by Dr. Colgan on 16 children with learning and behavioral difficulties, each child had his or her individual nutrient needs determined. Half the children were then given supplements, while the others acted

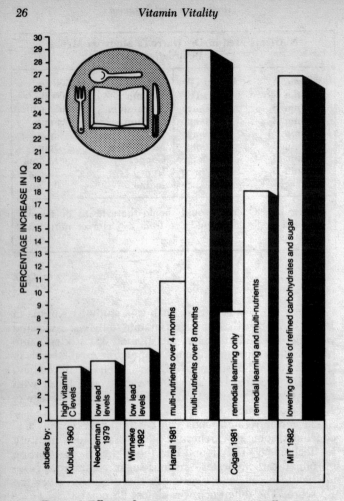

Figure 3 Effects of optimum nutrition on intelligence

as a control. Each child attended a remedial reading course designed to improve reading age by one year. Over the next 22 weeks teachers carefully monitored the reading age, IQ, and behavior of the children.

Those not taking supplements showed an average increase in IQ of 8.4 points and in reading age of 1.1 years. However, the group on supplements had an improvement in IQ of 17.9 points and their reading age went up by 1.8 years. The most likely explanation, Dr. Colgan concluded, was the decline in toxic levels of metals like lead, which are known to have detrimental effects on intelligence.[6]

A number of other studies have proved the connection between lead levels and intelligence.[7] One researcher, Dr. Needleman, who has tested thousands of children, has not yet found a single child with high lead who has an IQ above 125—normally, five percent of the population fall above this measurement. Since one in five children have some learning difficulties and that number continues to rise, it is vital that the role of nutrition as a powerful promoter of mental performance should be properly recognized.

The message is clear. Keep your vitamin nutrition to a maximum and pollution to a minimum and greater mental performance, memory, and emotional stability will result. Figure 3 summarizes the results of some of the studies that have proved the link between nutrition and intelligence.

Diet and Memory

The experience of an increase in mental alertness, ability to concentrate, and even in creativity is frequently reported by my clients. And without any doubt, one of the first areas to improve with optimum nutrition is memory.

A failing memory is one of the first signs of decreasing mental performance. Yet many people may never have had a very good memory in the first place. A survey of 87 clients showed that 53 percent were unable to recall their dreams. When we looked at clients under 30 years of age, 45 percent still had difficulty in recalling dreams. We all know that we dream during the night, but how many of us realize that we dream during the day too? When we are awake, we are not conscious of our "dream thoughts", since our conscious thoughts blot them out, just as the sun blots out the stars during the day. Dream recall is a useful measure of memory. It is likely that many people, young and old, have an impaired memory—for many, dream recall and memory will improve after six months of optimum nutrition.

Particularly important for memory are vitamins B_5, B_6, choline, manganese, and zinc. Rapid memory loss is a characteristic of senile dementia. It is often believed that memory always declines with age, but this isn't so: some people have an increasing memory and intelligence right up to the age of 90, although it is more common simply to maintain a good memory. However, one in five people over the age of 75 do suffer severe memory loss. According to Dr. Walford, 20 percent of senile dementia is caused by tiny hemorrhages or blood clots in the brain brought about by disease of the arteries.[8] But the cause of 50 to 60 percent of dementia is thought to be lack of a chemical called acetylcholine, used for nerve transmission in the brain. The nutrients needed to help the body produce more acetylcholine are the B vitamins pantothenic acid (B_5) and choline.[9]

Not surprisingly, we find that drugs that promote the production of acetylcholine, together with choline, help to restore and improve memory.[10] Choline, in doses of more than 10g a day, has been used to treat senile dementia.

Aluminium is often found in large amounts in those with impaired memory;[11] although the mechanism is as yet unknown, it may play an important role in the deterioration of memory. The brain chemical, spermine, is also found to be low in these cases. According to research at the Brain Bio Center in New Jersey, supplements of zinc and manganese, which elevate spermine, do appear to improve memory.

Diet, Crime, and Punishment

A president of a large company in the USA, with no previous history of law-breaking, goes for a drink in his local bar. For some reason he decides to have a glass of red wine, a drink he's never had before. Ten minutes later he pulls out a revolver and guns down a man walking past him. He shoots everyone who tries to help this man and ends up injuring 22 people. Miraculously, no one is killed, but many have serious wounds. A few hours later, in the local police station, he asks for a psychiatrist. "Why am I here?" he demands of him.

A man with 22 previous arrests for robbery and violence is released from prison. Within one week he walks past a police car parked at a gas station late one evening, places a stocking over his head and pulls out a gun. Going into the shop he says, "Put all your money in this bag or I'll blow your head off." Within minutes he is arrested. Crime psychologist Dr. Schauss asks him, "Didn't you see the police car in front of you?" He replies, "Yes, but there was no policeman in it." "Since when do the police leave their squad cars parked overnight in gas stations?" The man replies, "It's been the same every time, I make a stupid mistake like this!" This offender is an intelligent man; Schauss finds that he has an IQ of 140. With no chance of any sentence other than life imprisonment, why did he get himself arrested?

These are two seemingly cut-and-dried cases of people who, most would agree, should be locked away for our good. But each in its own way was a mystery, which Dr. Schauss, Director of the American Institute for Biosocial Research, only solved by considering nutritional as well as social factors.[12]

The company president was fortunate enough to be able to afford the best psychiatrists, neurologists, and doctors, but none could find out why he had carried out this atrocious crime. He was deeply horrified for having committed it, although he could not remember doing it. Dr. Schauss had the man screened for allergy—he had a very weakened immune system and showed the common allergic symptoms of rhinitis and headaches. He was then tested for sensitivity to various substances, including red wine—the likely offender if Dr. Schauss's theory was correct—with injection, sublingual drops, and ingestion, over a period of two months. But only Dr. Schauss knew that all he was actually being given were nonreactive "dummy" substances. After two months with no results,

Dr. Schauss then gave him exactly the same wine that he had drunk that fateful evening. Within ten minutes he became highly aggressive and increasingly violent, assaulting the nurse and tearing things apart in the laboratory. He was literally going through a metamorphosis, much like Jekyll and Hyde, and the psychiatrists present classified him as an acute paranoid schizophrenic.

Twelve years before this incident, the man had moved to a very expensive block of apartments in which a certain type of natural gas was used for heating and cooking. During the following year, most of the residents left their homes, even thought they had no chance of getting their money back, because of the health-damaging effects of the gas. This man had spent seven years there and it is likely that the gas had considerably weakened his immune system, contributing to an aggressive reaction most probably to a substance in the red wine. But the big question is: what sentence do you give this man who shot down and injured 22 people?

The second man did not have the money to spend on top specialists, but some interesting themes run through his criminal history. If you or I get a sudden impulse to steal a car or some money, before we take action we ask ourselves, "Is there a policeman near?" or "Will I be put in prison if I'm caught?" These simple inhibitory mechanisms come into play within microseconds of an impulse. Yet this man's behavior seemed to indicate that he had no "impulse control". Tests for food allergy revealed nothing, but a complete nutritional test showed that his iron level was well below normal.

The relevance of iron comes to light when we consider the chemistry of inhibition. In an emergency we release adrenaline and adrenaline-like substances that get us ready for action. One of the chemicals that inhibit adrenaline depends on iron to function. So a low iron level means low impulse control. This man, of much more than average intelligence, is now in prison for life, because each time he got an impulse to commit a crime, he may not have had the inhibitory signals that would have made him check if there was a policeman around, or ask whether it was really worth it. He knew the police car was there, but he didn't register its significance.

These two are not isolated cases, but ones that caught my attention because they indicate a new direction in attempts to solve our problem of an increasing rate of crime. Many factors have been proved to affect behavior— they include excess sugar, coffee, vitamin and mineral deficiencies, genetic effects and pollutants such as lead, as well as the social factors of poor schooling and disturbed family background. Even the color a room is painted has been shown to affect people's behavior. Yet society on the whole demands "an eye for an eye" and tougher punishment to get these problems under control—even though every time an adult is imprisoned we foot a bill in the USA of about $22,000 a year.

Between 1975 and 1980 400,000 people were in prison in the USA on any given day. This number is projected to rise to over 500,000 within the next five years. We now spend about $35,000 a year on keeping a juvenile in prison. Additionally, over one million former prisoners are currently on probation.[13] Is it not time to consider alternative approaches to treating criminals? After all, we used to lock away schizophrenics until we learned better—now they are beginning to be treated as people with real biochemical as well as psychological problems. The idea that people commit crimes because they had "bad parents" or were born with "bad genes" just does not hold up to the evidence. Often people commit crimes because they *feel* bad: unless we can find out what nutritional and environmental factors cause them to do so, how can we describe our penal system as just or effective?

Elemental Answers to Mental Illness

The brain is the most chemically sensitive part of the body. An excess of lead or a deficiency of vitamin C will affect the brain before any other organ.[14] Not surprisingly, as diet has become worse, an alarming number of people suffer from mental illnesses. Among the commonest of these are depression and anxiety, for which 124 million prescriptions—of tranquilizers, hypnotics, and antidepressants—are handed out every year in the United States. This is in a population of 209 million! Then there are schizophrenia, manic-depression, and obsessional neuroses. People suffering from mental illness fill more hospital beds than victims of any other diseases, including cancer and heart disease.

Since 1960 a group of expert doctors, biochemists, and nutritionists headed by Dr. Carl Pfeiffer have been exploring the role of nutrition in mental health. They founded the Brain Bio Center in New Jersey and have confirmed earlier work that suggested that schizophrenics have abnormal levels of certain brain chemicals. Earlier research had found that schizophrenics had higher levels of dopamine, a nerve-transmitter substance, and that some antipsychotic drugs block the release of dopamine. Another nerve-transmitter, serotonin, was also involved—the hallucinatory drug LSD, for example, produces its bizarre effects by interfering with the action of serotonin on the brain. Massive doses of vitamin B_3 provided relief in a number of cases.[15] It is now known that B_3 can raise serotonin levels. These results, however, were not consistent; some other factors appear to be involved. One of these is histamine, another nerve-transmitter substance.

Histamine, when oversupplied, causes tears to flow, noses to stream, and generally promotes the production of saliva and gastric juices—hay fever is a typical example of a histamine reaction. Histamine also protects us from stings and bites by causing swelling and isolating the poison. Our experience of pain is based on histamine, which protects us from burning or injuring ourselves. How does this relate to mental illness?

Dr. Carl Pfeiffer and his colleagues discovered that half the sufferers from schizophrenia they tested has unusually low levels of histamine, while 20 percent had high levels. Those with low levels responded well to vitamins B_3 and C, which raise the level of histamine. Those with high levels, of course, did not; instead they responded well to vitamin B_6, zinc,[16] and manganese.

Are You Histadelic?

All of us fall somewhere along the histamine range and you don't have to be schizophrenic to have a high histamine level. Those with high levels are "histadelic"; Dr. Pfeiffer describes them as "adapted for the twentieth century with a built-in self-destruct mechanism"! Histadelics are fast-living, fast-thinking individuals. They produce a lot of heat, and therefore tend to develop more pronounced facial features, have long fingers, and often have second toes longer than their big toes. They sweat a lot to dissipate their heat, and have prominent veins as a cooling mechanism. They are prone to colds, allergies, and headaches. Since they produce plenty of saliva their teeth are usually good; Marilyn Monroe, who remarked to photographers, "You always take pictures of my body but my most perfect feature is my teeth—I have no cavities", was probably histadelic. Histadelics are prone to depression, obsessions, and phobias—their suicide rate is far higher than that of those with low histamine levels. Most alcoholics are also high in histamine, since histadelics often try to dissipate their energy through drinking.

Those low in histamine are called "histapenic" and usually have a high level of the mineral copper. Often oversupplied from copper water pipes, this mineral is the second most common toxic metal after lead. Excess of copper can cause thought disorders, hallucinations, paranoia, and depression. The typical histapenic character tends to be resistant to colds, rarely allergic, often overweight, and also resistant to pain. Histapenics need more vitamin B_{12} and folic acid. Supplements of extra zinc and vitamin C are particularly important as they lower the copper level, helping to restore normal histamine balance.[17] Vitamin B_3 (niacin) is also important for correcting imbalances of histamine.

Many other nutritional factors have been found to be important in mental illnesses. The earliest discovery was that pellagra, which leads to psychosis, is caused by vitamin B_3 deficiency. Pellagra is now very rare in the west. The symptoms of deficiency in vitamin B_{12} or folic acid can mimic those of schizophrenia, while food and chemical allergies or sensitivities can bring on psychotic behavior or severe depression. In the near future vitamins, not drugs, will prove to be the psychiatrist's greatest ally.

4

Increasing Energy and Physical Performance

The chances are that your doctor has never seen a completely healthy person. Almost all medical research concerns itself only with ill people and disease. For this reason the world of athletics provides a unique chance to measure the effects of optimum nutrition on people who are supremely healthy.

For the athlete, excellent physical condition is the primary means to great achievements. Many top sportsmen and women follow special diets, take supplements,[1] and keep extremely fit and healthy. I certainly didn't expect to find signs of suboptimum vitamin deficiency among the athletes I tested, but to my surprise I did not find one *without* signs of nutritional deficiency. Since optimum nutrition improves the efficiency of muscle cells,[2] I wanted to test its effect on athletes, especially during endurance sports such as cycling or long-distance running.

Optimum Nutrition Improves Endurance

My first study was with a group of amateur racing cyclists.[3] Cycling, like long-distance running, is one of the harder endurance sports. We selected five cyclists, ranging from the age of 19 to 48. Each had a series of nutritional tests to calculate his or her optimum requirements and was then given supplement programs and dietary suggestions for a period of three months. Each was interviewed before and after by a nutritionist and a doctor. We monitored their best times over 25 miles before and after supplementation, and asked them to rate their own improvements subjectively in performance, recovery time, and health problems.

Their improvements in times ranged from a gain of 6½ minutes at one end to a loss of almost one minute at the other! But only one of the six registered a poorer time after supplementation; the other five all showed gains. The average gain over the six was more than 1½ minutes, reducing the time taken from 60½ minutes to just under 59 minutes.

The doctors' and cyclists' own comments are revealing. Here are some of them:

Doctors' reports: "Feels more alert. Also thinks he sleeps better." "Recovery time after races is better." "Undoubtedly racing better. Feels less tired and more alert and positive."

Cyclists' reports: "I feel fresher, my times have improved." "My cycling performance is better and my recovery rate after races is tremendous."

One of the cyclists even noted after taking the vitamin supplements he was no longer allergic to coffee; another, a woman, experienced a marked improvement in the degree of premenstrual tension that she usually suffered.

My results confirmed the earlier findings of Dr. Colgan, who had tested the effects of nutrition on marathon runners.[4] There is little doubt that optimum nutrition does improve endurance, although these findings are all very recent and need to be confirmed by further research. The effects of optimum nutrition would also be much more pronounced after six months to a year, than after only three months.

Good Nutrition Makes You Strong

What have Sylvester Stallone, star of *Rocky*, and Christopher Reeve, alias *Superman*, got in common? They both take a careful balance of nutritional supplements to maintain their Goliath-like strength. Optimum nutrition has been shown to increase not only endurance, but also sheer muscle-power. The effect is best illustrated in a study by Dr. Colgan in which four experienced weight lifters were split into two groups. One group was given a special supplement program, tne other placebos. After three months, those on supplements had increased the maximum weight they could lift by about 50 percent. The others, on dummy tablets, had only 10 to 20 percent increase. During the following three months, the supplements and the placebos were swapped around. Those previously on placebos caught up with the other weight lifters.[5]

For us mere mortals, vitamins really do give us increased vitality and energy. Lack of energy should be considered a disease. More of my clients complain of flagging energy than of any other symptom. For example, when Liz H. first saw me she was exhausted after a nine A.M. to four P.M. job. "My husband wouldn't talk to me till at least six P.M. I was grumpy, exhausted and often fell asleep. Since being on the vitamin program I'm able to work from eight A.M. to five P.M. and I come home feeling wide awake. My husband and I get on much better, too!"

Although measuring energy is difficult, we all know the difference between feeling vital and alive, and tired and lethargic. From my own experience with hundreds of clients, I know that increased energy is the first sign of improvement. At least three-quarters of all the people I treat notice their energy and vitality improving within the first four to eight weeks of starting their personal health program—an effect that is also reported by people who start doing regular physical exercise. Although we have a lot to learn about the chemistry of well-being, it is likely that this effect is partly due to an increased rate of metabolism and to the production of certain nerve-chemicals in the body. One group of chemicals, called endorphins,[6] are thought to act as natural "highs", making us feel happy and alert. It is known that vitamin C increases the production of endorphins. So do exercise—and music! Now you know why joggers listening to personal stereos are always smiling!

Keeping a Healthy Heart

With cardiovascular disease (cardio = heart; vascular = to do with the circulation, i.e. veins and arteries) being the number one killer in the west today, our attention is inevitably drawn to the role of nutrition and exercise. Both

have been shown to help, but neither appears to provide
all the answers. Jim Fixx, the famous author of *The
Complete Book of Running*, died at the age of 52 from a
heart attack while jogging. The autopsy found that two of
his coronary arteries were almost totally clogged, which is
not so surprising to those who knew of his disregard for
dietary advice. On the other hand, the heart surgeon, Dr.
Albert Starr, an advocator of the low-cholesterol diet,
needed open-heart surgery at only 47 years of age. Having
performed the very same operation over 3,000 times, he
had followed all the guidelines for staying free of heart
disease.

Which is more important, diet or exercise? Bill Solomon
from the University of Arizona designed an experiment to
find out the answer.[7] He got some obliging pigs to run
around a track, but fed them the average vitamin-deficient
diet. Another group ate the pig-equivalent of health food
but had no exercise; and a third group had both exercise
and good nutrition. The third group of pigs fared best,
proving that exercise and good nutrition together are vital
for optimum health.

Your pulse rate is the simplest means to keep a check on
the health of your strongest muscle, the heart. A fast
resting pulse rate of 100 beats per minute reflects a weak
heart, which has to beat frequently to keep your blood
flowing through the arteries and veins. On the other hand,
a resting pulse of 50 beats per minute, the average for
good marathon runners, represents a heart that is twice as
strong. The "normal" pulse rate is set at 72 beats per
minute, although for someone leading a sedate life-style a
pulse of 65 would be nearer the ideal. The resting pulse
rate should not go up substantially with age. For example,
my pulse was 72 at the age of 18 and is now 60, with my
exercise level remaining the same. This is consistent with
the findings by other researchers on the effects of nutrition. One study found that the average pulse rate of 18
women dropped from 76 to 68 beats per minute after six
months of optimum nutrition.[8]

While it used to be thought that the fatty deposits that
casue the arteries to narrow were the result of excess

cholesterol in the diet and hence in the blood, recent evidence suggests a different explanation. Arterial deposits form only in certain parts of the circulation system. It appears that the cells in the artery wall in these areas begin to overmultiply, a bit like cancer cells, and eventually break through into the artery. This lesion then attracts cholesterol and calcium even if your blood cholesterol level is low. One of the major causes of such cell proliferation is damage caused by "free radicals", by-products of oxygen (these are explained in more detail in Chapter 5). Vitamins C and E and the mineral selenium help detoxify these free radicals, and are therefore crucial additions in a diet for a healthy heart.

Monitoring Your Blood Pressure

Your blood pressure is a measure of the health of your arteries. Every time your heart beats, the pressure in your arteries reaches a maximum. Then there is a lull before the next beat. The maximum pressure is your "systolic" pressure and the minimum is your "diastolic" pressure. These are written with the systolic pressure first, followed by the diastolic: for example, 120/80. Blood pressures greater than this example can indicate the beginnings of narrowing or hardening of the arteries. A blood pressure of 150/95 is getting serious. The old "rule of thumb" of allowing your systolic blood pressure to be 100 plus your age (i.e. 160 if you are 60 years old) is inaccurate. With good nutrition and exercise, your blood pressure should reduce to below 130/90, considerably decreasing your risk of cardiovascular disease.

Since raised blood pressure is usually the result of the formation of deposits in the arteries over many years, it rarely comes down substantially even after six months of nutritional treatment. After four years, however, one group of men with a marginally high blood pressure of 140/90 had reduced this to 120/80 without any drugs or increase in exercise.[8] A level of 120/80 represents a very low risk of cardiovascular disease. But blood levels of cholesterol and triglycerides, which are associated with high risk,[9] have been shown to reduce substantially in as little as three months. Contrary to popular belief, the dietary intake of cholesterol has little to do with the level of cholesterol in the blood.[10] There is remarkably little substantial evidence to show that a diet low in fats, but high in cholesterol, is in any way associated with heart disease.[11] However, there is no doubt that reducing our intake of saturated fats can only be beneficial.

Have a look at the "Heart Check" on page 94. If you score five or more, your personal health program will need to include extra nutrients to strengthen your cardiovascular health. Changes in your life-style, such as the inclusion of regular exercise, not smoking, reducing your consumption of alcohol,[12] meat,[13] sugar,[14] and salt[15] are highly recommended. Vitamins C and B_3[16] improve cardiovascular health and vitamin E is essential for preventing blood clots and transporting cholesterol.[17] The minerals calcium,[18] magnesium,[19] and potassium[20] are also very important. Potassium is best obtained from the diet by increasing your consumption of fresh fruit. Calcium and magnesium are highest in seeds and nuts, but extra supplements are usually also needed.

5

Life Span: Secrets for Staying Young

The quest for immortality or, at least, extended life span is nothing new. Since the beginning of history, myths and legends about magic potions and ancient men have abounded. But now, as we approach the twenty-first century, many scientists and gerontologists (gerontology is the study of aging) are predicting that a life span of 120 will soon be possible. For some, extended life span means prolonged old age and more years of misery. For others, it is deemed unnatural or not "the will of God".

But aging is not a function of time. Certainly they go together, but that does not mean that the passage of time *causes* one to age. After all, a 50-year-old man can have a biological age of 30 or 70. Why the difference? Nor are most deaths "natural". Over 75 percent of deaths are caused by diseases like cancer, heart disease, bronchial infections, or accidents. Would it not be preferable if we could live our entire and extended life in optimum health until the day we died?

What Is the Maximum Life Span?

To understand the science of life extension, many different questions must be asked. What is the known maximum achieved life span? What are the necessary conditions for living long? What happens when we age? What are the major causes of death, and can these be prevented? And lastly, how can we extend the maximum?

According to gerontologist Dr. Walford, it is unlikely that anyone has lived to be 120 years old. Most claims for longevity cannot be proved beyond a doubt. For example, Attila the Hun (died A.D. 500) was supposed to have lived to 121, and Jonathon Hartrop (died 1791), from the Yorkshire village of Aldbrough, was said to have attained the ripe old age of 138. However, birth and death records are simply not good enough to substantiate such claims. More recent records of the Hunzas, an Indian tribe, and inhabitants of the Caucasus in the USSR, are also likely to be exaggerations. For example, one villager was reported in the Soviet papers to be 130—until his fellow villagers identified him as a deserter in World War I, who had used his father's papers to avoid being returned to the front. In fact, he was only 78. What fame is there in being an aged 78? But to be 130 immediately makes one noble, a celebrity. "The oldest person with fully acceptable credentials was Fanny Thomas, who lived to be 113 years and 215 days and died in April, 1980, in San Gabriel, California. [She attributed] her longevity to the fact that she ate apple sauce three times a day and never married, so 'never had a man to bother me'."[1]

With the exception of the tortoise, which can live to be 150, human beings are the longest living mammals.

What Is the Average Life Span?

Contrary to popular belief, there has been little change in the average life span in the last 60 years. At the bottom end of the scale, vast increases in general sanitation and preventative approaches to infectious and contagious diseases such as smallpox have dramatically improved our chances of survival early in life. Our average life expectancy is now 74 while forty years ago it was 72. Few of us are still alive at the age of 100, and even fewer at our current maximum of about 113. The major reason for this is not infectious disease, but degenerative diseases such as cancer and cardiovascular diseases—and, of course, accidents.

Increasing the 50-Percent Survival Rate

The first major breakthrough in aging has already begun: it is the decrease in deaths due to cardiovascular disease. Accounting for over 40 percent of deaths in the 1970s but only 12 percent in 1900, it is logical to assume that strokes (blockages in the arteries at the base of the head) and heart disease have come about through something we are doing that we were not doing 100 years ago. Along with a decline in overall fitness,[2] we now have increased consumption of sugar,[3] fat[4] and refined foods[5] (causing a lower intake of vitamins and minerals), increased smoking,[6] and increased exposure to environmental pollution and chemicals in our food. Too often we accept the death of a relative or friend as an "act of God" or bad luck. But there is no element of chance involved in cardiovascular disease, which has now reached epidemic proportions. In the nineteenth century the same views were held about the contagious diseases until the causes for these were understood and later eradicated. And many of the factors listed above are also responsible for our increased rate of cancer.

Preventing the Major Killers with Optimum Nutrition

I have already mentioned the role of vitamins C and E and the mineral selenium in the prevention of heart disease; vitamins against cancer is my next concern. Cancer cells are cells that continue to divide and multiply, like our own cells do during development in the womb. This unruly cellular behavior occurs either because environmental factors (carcinogens) damage the cell's internal behavior code (its DNA), or by natural errors of metabolism. Every day cancer cells are produced and begin to multiply, but fortunately we have an efficient "hit squad" called the immune system. The cells of the immune system carry out 24-hour surveillance on these misfit cells and destroy them before it's too late. However, if the immune system isn't strong enough, the cancer cells keeps multiplying and protect themselves from the immune system. A cell mass that doesn't spread is called a benign tumor. One that continues to grow is called a carcinoma (if it is in epithelial tissue—the inner or outer skin of the body, such as lung or colon), a sarcoma (if it is in supporting structures like fibrous tissue), leukemia (if it is in blood-forming cells), or lymphoma (if it is in lymph nodes). These are all forms of cancer.

With nutrition, we have three lines of defense. The first involves the prevention of DNA damage; the second, the strengthening of the immune system, and the third, the avoidance or neutralization of carcinogens. One of the major causes of cell damage is the behavior of free radicals. A free radical is an atom or group of atoms with an uneven electrical charge. To complete itself it steals a charged particle (an electron) from a neighboring cell, which can set up a chain of reactions producing more free radicals, damaging more cells and causing them to misbehave. Many normal chemical reactions, such as breathing in oxygen and turning it into carbon dioxide, give rise to the formation of free radicals. Unsaturated oils, such as vegetable oils, are particularly susceptible to free radical damage, especially when heated. So we have developed ways of dealing with these by-products of using oxygen. These are antioxidants.

Antioxidants, like vitamin C and vitamin E, protect our cells from free radical attack. Both have been shown to increase life span.[7] Nuts and seeds also contain vitamin E to protect their essential oils from oxidation, which is the same as rancidity. Yet some oil manufacturers remove vitamin E and sell us vegetable oil that is prone to rancidity.

We also have enzymes designed to disarm free radicals. One of these, SOD (superoxide dismutase), is at the forefront of both cancer and cardiovascular research, which has led to the sale of SOD tablets in health food shops. Yet there is little evidence that SOD taken in tablets can survive the perils of digestion and remain intact to strengthen us from the aging effect of oxides. One type of SOD, however, which is dependent on the presence of manganese, may explain why supplements of manganese decrease the incidence of sarcoma cancers in rats.[8] Another SOD depends on an careful balance of copper and zinc. An excess of copper or a deficiency of zinc have also been shown to be associated with increased cancers.[9]

A close relative antioxidant enzyme, GP (glutathione peroxidase), depends on the mineral selenium. Increase the dietary intake of selenium by a factor of ten and you will double the activity of GP.[10] In both animals and man high selenium is associated with low risk of cancer.[11] In one study 111 patients who developed cancer within a five-year period were compared to a group of 210 people who remained cancer-free. The selenium level in the cancer victims was significantly lower. Those with very low selenium levels had double the chance of getting cancer compared to those with very high selenium levels. Also, parts of the world rich in selenium have typically low rates of breast cancer.[12] On the basis of this, and extensive animal studies, I take 50 mcg of selenium every day.

Strengthening the White Army

The immune system is like an army of cells, with a mission to seek out and destroy invaders. Invaders can be viruses, bacteria, or cancer cells, all of which are recognized as alien. Our army consists of white blood cells that can be broken down into smaller units. These include macrophages, which gather round inflamed or infected areas and gobble up foreign particles, and lymphocytes. B-lymphocytes help produce antibodies that are specifically designed to destroy the invaders or antigens. Another type, called "natural killer" lymphocytes, are particularly good at destroying cancer cells. Of course, these cells are themselves very destructive and their numbers must be controlled. T-lymphocytes are designed to do this job. But none of these works without an adequate supply of vitamins.[13]

To have maximum protection from infection, you need to be able to produce the antibodies specifically geared to the invading organism. This system forms the basis of inoculation: a small amount of flu virus, for example, enables your white army to produce its antibodies for defense next time. Deficiency of vitamins B_2, B_5 (pantothenic acid), and B_6 have all been shown to decrease antibody production.[14] Lymphocytes become less active when folic acid or B_{12} levels are low.[15] B vitamins support your white army, protecting you from cancer cells and strengthening you against viruses.

The most common virus is the common cold. Thanks to the work of Dr. Linus Pauling, the widespread use of vitamin C supplements helps provide protection.[16] Yet every year the vitamin C controversy continues to rage in the medical journals. Many studies have shown no effect, while others support Dr. Pauling's claims. But a closer examination of the studies that show no effect from vitamin C usually reveal either that less than 1,000mg is used, or that the poor subjects of the experiment are artificially exposed to a massive amount of cold virus, quite out of proportion to the level of exposure we are designed to deal with. After all, it is no good treating a headache with a hundredth of an aspirin, nor is it any good treating a fully-blown migraine attack with two aspirins. The dosage level is crucial. At the right dosage—usually 1,000mg or more—vitamin C increases the production of antibodies as well as having other strengthening properties for our immune system.[17] In animals it increases T-lymphocytes, which control the levels of other lymphocytes.[18] The other antioxidant vitamin, vitamin E, is an even stronger booster of the white army. Large amounts of vitamin E can double or triple antibody formation, while deficiency can reduce antibody formation to zero![19]

Detoxifying Carcinogens

Asbestos and cigarette smoke are well-known carcinogens, but there are more than 5,000 other substances known to promote cancer. Among these, nitrosamines, nitrates, and nitrites are particularly prevalent.[20] The worldwide use of artificial fertilizers has caused a massive increase in the amount of nitrates we consume in our food. If hydrochloric acid levels are low, or vitamin C absent, nitrates, in turn, can combine in the digestive tract to form the highly carcinogenic nitrosamines.[21] Recently, there has been a suggestion that low vitamin A levels are associated with a high risk of lung cancer and this has highlighted the role of vitamin A in protecting the "inside skin" of the lungs and digestive tract from carcinogens.[22]

A three-pronged attack against cancer and aging must involve nutrients to strengthen the immune system (vitamins B_2, B_5, B, and B_{12}; folic acid; vitamins C and E; and zinc); nutrients to protect us from cellular damage (vitamins C and E, and zinc, manganese, and selenium), and nutrients to detoxify carcinogens (vitamins C and A). Chapter 9 gives you guidelines for assessing your personal requirements for these.

Accidents and Aging

In nature, far more deaths occur through accidents than from any other cause. The most common accident is getting eaten—one which we need fear no longer. Some organisms, such as sea anemones, do not age: their population is kept under control entirely through accidents. For mankind, accidents account for six percent of all deaths, nearly half of these involving motor vehicles. This accident rate is more than double that at the beginning of the century and is probably the result of a changing physical environment, involving crowded towns, many more cars on the roads, staircases, and slippery baths. For many elderly people a slip in the bath or a fall down the stairs marks the beginning of pneumonia or flu. More stringent safety controls and better technology for older people should help reduce death through accidents in the future.

Once we've avoided the accidents, and prevented the degenerative diseases such as hardening of the arteries and cancer, why then do we age? One theory, known as the Hayflick limit, suggests that our cells are preprogramed to self-destruct.[23] Within the nucleus of each cell ticks away a time bomb; when time runs out, the cell dies. While a substantial amount of evidence supports this theory (for example, if you put a new nucleus in an old cell, the cell lives longer), it is unlikely that this explanation is the whole story.

A brilliant piece of research suggested another mechanism, based on the rate of repair of our "blueprint for survival", the DNA molecule.[24] The DNA molecule contains the information to build new and healthy cells. Since we build some billions of cells every day, the accuracy of our DNA is crucial. Yet DNA is itself often damaged by normal chemical reactions in the body, as well as by radiation, cigarette smoke, and other environmental pollutants. By comparing the rate of repair of DNA in different species of animals, the researchers found that those that repaired DNA most rapidly lived longest. Since one of the principal causes of DNA damage is the action of free radicals, antioxidants like vitamins C and E are seen to be essential for a healthy life span.

Another sign of aging is a weakened immune system. The immune system is designed to recognize anything that is not "us" and destroy it. For example, when we are exposed to a virus, the immune system is activated to produce macrophages and lymphocytes, which attach to and gobble up the invading virus. As we age, our immune system weakens. With that, the ability to fight off infections and keep cancer cells at bay declines. With more than 17 percent of deaths coming from cancer, and nearly 4 percent from pneumonia, flu, or bronchial infections, strengthening the immune system is vital.

But the immune system doesn't always go wrong by becoming bad at its job. Sometimes it attacks itself. SLE (systematic lupus erythematosus), an autoimmune disease, serves as a good example of a disease in which the victim produces antibodies that destroy its own cells. Optimum nutrition can help here as well. My first client with SLE was under close surveillance because she produced so many self-destructive antibodies. After 12 months of optimum nutrition her antibody count had dropped dramatically and all her symptoms were gone.

Many diseases whose symptoms include signs of rapid aging show the same autoimmune response. Perhaps our cellular pacemaker is programed to end life through this form of self-destruction. Salmon do something like this, using hormones. After four years in the open sea, salmon find their way back to the place where they were born where, after spawning, their adrenal glands release a massive amount of hormones. The fish age within minutes to the point of death.

Examination of the various theories of aging shows that a possible human life span of more than 100 years is far from an illusion. By making healthy cells, preventing and repairing DNA damage, and optimizing the health of your immune system, life span can be pushed to the limits.

Eat Less and Live Longer

Improving our nutrition isn't the only thing we can do to stay young. Exercise and *undernutrition* are also important keys. A 300-percent increase in life span through calorie restriction has been found in fish,[19] and a 60-percent increase in rats.[25] Calorie restriction—undernutrition—is not the same as malnutrition. The evidence is clear: keep the calories low, but the quality of nutrition high. These studies,[26] involving severe calorie restriction, have not been carried out on man for obvious ethical reasons. Yet it is more likely that the leaner you are the longer you'll live. With today's diet that means low fat and sugar and extra vitamin supplements. But be careful. Crash diets are especially inadvisable and are not the best way to live longer, or to lose weight (see p. 67). Calorie reduction should be a very gradual process. Many of my clients in fact lose weight on optimum nutrition programs without even trying, because optimum nutrition leaves one craving less and eating less.

Exercise Keeps You Young

Regular exercise can add seven years to your life span, concludes Drs. Rose and Cohen of the Veterans' Administration Hospital in Boston. But the exercise must be continued late into life and must be "aerobic"—i.e. your heart rate must reach 80 percent of its maximum for at least twenty minutes. Cycling, swimming, and running are good; on the other hand, weightlifting, yoga, and strengthening exercises do little to extend your life. Aerobic exercise reduces blood cholesterol levels,[27] pulse and blood pressure, promoting better cardiovascular health as well as increasing mental function. It also helps you maintain proper blood sugar control thereby especially helping diabetics.[28] For more on aerobic exercise, see Chapter 11.

The Not Too Distant Future

No one knows for sure what breakthrough in life extension will occur in the next 30 years. But given what we know now, life span can be extended by at least ten years through optimum nutrition, even if you start late in life. The experts are certainly optimistic.

"The long-term effects of optimum nutrition are at least an extra ten years of healthful living," says Dr. Carl Pfeiffer, aged 77, who had a massive heart attack at 51. The lone survivor of a family of five children, he takes at least 10g of vitamin C a day to help prevent cancer. He works 14 hours a day at the Brain Bio Center and intends to keep doing so for at least another ten years. He is energetic and alert, and still enjoys excellent hearing and eyesight. "Provided you are not in the grip of a degenerative disease already, you are likely to get at least a decade of vigorous years, and perhaps a lot more, added to your life, no matter what age you are now," says Dr. Michael Colgan. Biochemically, he is no older now than he was 11 years ago, when he started researching the effects of optimum nutrition. "It seems fairly certain that maximum life span could already be prolonged to 130 or 140 years by the exercise of very stringent measures," says Dr. Roy Walford, leading gerontologist.[29] Nobel prize winner Dr. Linus Pauling, aged 83, believes that optimum nutrition with extra vitamin C could add 16 to 24 years to the average life span. Dr. Roger Williams, aged 91, sometimes called the father of optimum nutrition, says: "Well-rounded nutrition, including generous amounts of vitamins C and E, can contribute materially to extending the healthy life span of those who are already middle-aged. The greatest hope for increasing life spans can be offered if nutrition—from the time of prenatal development to old age—is continuously of the highest quality."

6

Fertility, Pregnancy, and Menstrual Health

One in every four couples suffers from some degree of infertility.[1] For some, this means having fewer children than they want; for most, it means no children at all. And for couples who are fertile, getting pregnant is not the easy matter that it is commonly thought to be. The average length of time taken to get pregnant is six months, although 18 months is not uncommon.[2] Unless fertility tests show otherwise, failure to conceive within 18 months does not necessarily mean that you are completely infertile.

Fertility and the speed of conception depend on many factors, some psychological, some physical, and some nutritional. Conceptions are very high during holiday periods, for example, since stress—a major factor in infertility—is reduced. Knowing how to time intercourse to coincide with ovulation (the release of the female egg to be fertilized by the sperm) greatly increases the chances of conception. Also, your nutrition and especially your vitamin status play a crucial role.

Vitamins for Fertility

The male is responsible in about a third of infertility cases. It should be stressed that infertility has nothing to do with sexual virility, which is usually not affected. The usual test for infertility in a man involves a sperm count—the higher the sperm count, the greater the fertility. A recent study has shown that extra vitamin C increased sperm count as well as sperm mobility, but exactly why this is so is not yet known.[3] Likewise, vitamin E deficiency has been found to induce sterility in both sexes by causing damage to the reproductive tissues. Unfortunately, however, simply taking vitamin E will not reverse the condition if you are sterile.[4]

The high rate of infertility among diabetics may provide us with a clue. Diabetics are frequently low in vitamin A, which is essential for making the male sex hormones. Vitamin A is dependent on zinc to be released from the liver. Of all the nutrients known to affect male fertility, zinc is perhaps the best researched. Signs of zinc deficiency include late sexual maturation, small sex organs, and infertility. With adequate supplements of zinc these problems can be corrected. Dr. Carl Pfeiffer has also found a high degree of impotence and infertility in his male patients who suffer from zinc deficiency. "With adequate dosage of vitamin B_6 and zinc," he writes, "the sexual ability of the male should return in one or two months' time."[5] In view of the fact that the average dietary intake of zinc has been found to be substantially lower at 7.9mg than the intake of 15mg recommended by the National Research Council,[6] the effects of zinc on fertility may be quite substantial and widespread. Zinc is found in high concentrations in the sex glands of the male and also the sperm itself. There it is needed to make the outer layer and the tail and is therefore essential for healthy sperm. As such as 1.4mg of zinc is lost with each ejaculation, so a prolific sex life and an inadequate diet would put you at risk! In the nineteenth century many patients were diagnosed as having "masturbation insanity"—perhaps the earliest suggestion of a link between zinc, sex, and mental illness. There may be more than an element of truth in the old saying that masturbation makes you blind and stunts your growth, since both of these are signs of zinc deficiency!

For women, zinc is also crucial. Problems of fertility, sex drive, and menstruation have all been linked to inadequate levels of zinc. The sex hormone, gonadotrophin, needs zinc and vitamin B_6 to be produced in adequate quantities. Vitamin B_6 together with zinc beneficially affect every part of the female sexual cycle. They increase desire for sex, alleviate premenstrual problems, ease sickness in pregnancy and postnatal depression, and increase the chances of a healthy baby.

Contraception: Pros and Cons

It is not just dietary deficiency that can cause problems with zinc and vitamin B_6, but also the birth control pill. The link was discovered when 80mg of B_6 helped those suffering from depression induced by the pill.[7] The pills also induces deficiencies in vitamin C and the B vitamins,[8] especially B_{12}.[9] Since the pill also elevates the level of copper,[10] which has been associated with increased birth defects, one might end up taking ten vitamin and mineral pills to counteract the effects of this contraceptive! A much better alternative is to switch to a safer form of birth control: since the use of the pill has been associated with migraine headaches, cervical cancer, and an increase in depression and suicide among young women. Medical researcher and gynecologist Dr. Ellen Grant says, "Women have been sacrificed to the god of perfect contraception", and advises strongly against the pill. Unfortunately, its effects do not stop when you cease taking it; the chance of having an abnormal baby has already been increased from 0.9 to 4.3 percent.[11] Also, a greater incidence of allergies is now being discovered among children of mothers who used to take the pill.[12] Not surprisingly, fertility is also affected. So what are the alternatives?

The coil or IUD (intrauterine device) is also not ideal. Many types of coil are made from copper and these greatly elevate levels of this toxic metal in the body. Since copper is a strong enemy of zinc, zinc deficiency is greatly increased. Copper is the second most common toxic mineral, so any potential sources of extra copper are best avoided. Non-copper IUDs do not present this problem.

Natural Methods of Birth Control

Unlike the pill or coil, natural methods of birth control do not interfere with the cycle of ovulation (the release of the egg from the ovary) and menstruation (the discharge of the nourishing part of the uterus in which a fertilized egg would implant). During this cycle, which can vary from 23 to 35 days,[13] there is only one day in which the egg is available for fertilization. This is the point of ovulation. However, sperm usually live for three days; under excellent conditions, they can survive for five days (a longer survival rate is extremely rare). If one knew exactly when ovulation occurred, abstinence from sex for five days (or the use of diaphragm or condom) would reduce the chance of pregnancy, while frequent sex during this time would dramatically increase it. How, then, do you find out when ovulation occurs?

The ways to find out can be briefly summarized in three groups. Perhaps the best known is the rhythm method, which predicts ovulation a certain number of days after menstruation every month, but this is not a method to be recommended to those whose cycle is not absolutely regular.[14] The temperature method depends on taking the body temperature at different times of the month, since it rises after ovulation due to an increase in the hormone progesterone. The disadvantage of this method is that it can only tell you *after* ovulation has occurred: it cannot predict it in advance.

A third method, simple and apparently a breakthrough, is expounded by Dr. E. Billings in her book, *The Billings Method* (Random House, 1980). It is based on the discovery that a different type of vaginal mucus is produced just before ovulation. If you can learn to recognize this accurately, you will know just when to avoid intercourse if you do not want to become pregnant and, of course, just when you are most fertile if you are trying for a child. Most researchers report a success rate of 97 to 99 percent using this method of birth control, provided that intercourse is abstained from for just a few days in each cycle.

Choosing the Sex of Your Child

In the 1960s it was thought that the "male" sperm had different characteristics from the "female" sperm, making it a better swimmer. The sex of the embryo was therefore thought to be influenced by the timing of intercourse: the nearer ovulation, the greater the likelihood of a boy. But this theory is not supported by fact and some other studies have found the opposite effect.

A more plausible and well-researched approach was put forward in 1967 by Professor Stolwoski. He had found that the sex of calves correlated with the levels of certain minerals in the mother's feed. The more calcium and magnesium he fed his cows, the more females were born. On the other hand, the more sodium and potassium, the more male calves were born. He tested his theories in one study in which 49 cows were treated with the "female diet", high in calcium and magnesium and low in sodium and potassium, and 380 were untreated. The untreated cows produced 43 percent females, while the treated ones produced 63.3 percent females.

In 1975 two doctors followed up this work by examining the diets of 100 women who had children of only one sex. Once more, 80 percent of those with boys only had a diet high in salt and low in calcium and magnesium, while 80 percent of those with girls only had a diet low in salt and high in calcium and magnesium.

This approach has since been researched and written up by Françoise Labro and Dr. Papa in *Boy or Girl?* (Souvenir Press, 1984), who claim a 78 percent success rate for those who have followed their special diets for choosing a boy or a girl. But *why* does it work? In all honesty nobody knows. Dr. Papa thinks that diet may affect the ovum's preference for a male or female sperm. Dr. Pfeiffer's findings, however, may suggest a different conclusion.

At the Brain Bio Center in New Jersey, Dr. Pfeiffer and his colleagues treat many patients with low zinc levels. They soon discovered that low zinc was associated with a high rate of female births, and that mothers with all girl families were likely to be zinc deficient. Since the male fetus is more dependent upon zinc, this could be explained by a greater number of aborted male fetuses in women low in zinc. (On average, one in three fertilized eggs is aborted in the first month, which is why pregnancy tests are best carried out after one month.)

Dr. Pfeiffer also found that people with low histamine levels (histapenics) were more likely to be low in zinc and high in copper. The high histamine types (histadelics), on the other hand, did not show such mineral imbalances. What does this have to do with calcium and magnesium levels? The answer is that both these minerals lower histamine levels[15] and are therefore used to treat histadelic patients. So a diet high in calcium and magnesium would be more likely to result in a girl, especially among mothers already low in histamine.

It is interesting to note that research carried out by Professor Bryce-Smith[16] is beginning to show that aborted fetuses tend to be high in cadmium, lead, or copper and low in zinc. Cadmium, lead, and copper are all zinc antagonists so these preliminary findings do at least suggest that zinc status is crucial for fetal development. Perhaps the male's need for extra zinc is enough to tip the scales in favor of a girl for mothers with low zinc levels.

Vitamins for a Healthy Pregnancy

While only time will tell whether nutrition is a deciding factor in the sex of your child, there is no doubt that optimum nutrition can greatly improve your chances of having a healthy pregnancy. Even the slightest deficiencies during pregnancy can have serious effects on the health of the offspring,[17] and the idea that birth defects are often caused by nutritional imbalances in the mother is rapidly gaining wider acceptance. So far, slight deficiencies of vitamin B_1, B_2, B_6,[18] folic acid,[19] zinc,[20] iron, calcium,[21] and magnesium[22] have all been linked to birth abnormalities. So too have excesses of toxic metals, especially lead,[23] cadmium,[24] and copper. Severe deficiencies of any vitamin will cause birth abnormalities, since a vitamin by definition is necessary for maintaining normal growth. Naturally, a healthy pregnancy will depend on a greater supply than normal of all these nutrients since the needs of a growing fetus, together with her own needs, put extra demands on the expectant mother.

As many as five percent of births show some developmental defect,[25] many of which affect the central nervous system. Spina bifida, a condition in which the neural tube doesn't develop properly, affects one child in 10,000 in the United States. It has been strongly linked to a lack of folic acid in the mother's diet and probably of other nutrients too. The incidence of this condition is far higher where mothers have had a nutritionally poor diet for the first three months of pregnancy.[26] One study found that dietary counseling alone did lower the rate of spina bifida in those mothers at risk, but that the administration of extra folic acid, on its own or in a multivitamin preparation, resulted in a much lower number of babies with neural tube defects.[27] Since the recommended folic acid intake is 400mcg per day and the average intake is between 100 to 200mcg per day, a supplement of 200mcg per day is recommended for those intending to become pregnant.

During the first three months of pregnancy all the organs of the body are completely formed. It is during this period—and, of course, before—that optimum nutrition is most important. Yet many women experience continual sickness and don't feel like eating healthily. Misnamed "morning" sickness, this condition has been accepted as normal during the first three months of pregnancy. Probably due to increases in a hormone called HCG, women with poor diets are particularly at risk. During pregnancy the need for vitamin B_6, B_{12}, folic acid, iron, and zinc all increase; extra supplements of these usually stop even the worst cases of pregnancy sickness. Eating small, frequent amounts of fruit or complex carbohydrates like nuts, seeds, or wholegrains often helps. However, the best approach is to ensure optimum nutrition well before pregnancy. We followed up four women on optimum nutrition programs before and during pregnancy—the average number of days in which nausea or sickness was reported was two days. Yet for some women nausea continues throughout the entire pregnancy!

Another common complication of pregnancy is called

preeclamptic toxemia, consisting of an increase in blood pressure, edema (swelling), and an excess level of protein in the urine. Many theories abound as to why this occurs, but once more optimum nutrition is a vital factor. One of my clients who had had preeclamptic toxemia during her previous pregnancy improved her diet and added nutritional supplements: her second pregnancy was entirely healthy and she didn't even experience nausea.

For the mother, optimum nutrition before and during pregnancy ensures a healthier pregnancy with fewer complications, resulting in a healthier and heavier baby.[28] Apart from following the vitality diet (Chapter 10) and working out your personal health program (Chapter 9), your supplement program should include 200mcg of folic acid, 20mcg of vitamin B_{12}, 200mg of vitamin B_6, 15 mg of zinc, 500mg of calcium, 250mg of magnesium, and 12mg of iron. Do not take more than 20,000IU of vitamin A, and have a hair mineral analysis to check for excesses of copper, lead, or cadmium.

PMT—The Curse That Can Be Cured

Premenstrual problems were, until relatively recently, accepted as a woman's lot. Yet these symptoms—which include depression, tension, headaches, breast tenderness, bloatedness, low energy, and irritability—are in most cases avoidable. Classically, they occur in the week preceding menstruation, though a small percentage of women have the symptoms from the middle of the cycle, coinciding with ovulation. Since premenstrual problems are a result of hormonal changes, hormone treatment has been used to correct them. But the use of such drug treatment must be seriously questioned as it does disrupt the body's chemistry and has been associated with a greater risk of cancer. The effectiveness of vitamin B_6 has now been proved to help 70 percent of premenstrual sufferers.[29] More recently, research has focused on the role of GLA (gamma linolenic acid), an essential fatty acid found in the oil of the evening primrose. GLA's high success rate of 60 percent is almost certainly due to its role in making prostaglandins, which are hormone-like substances in the body.[30] But why are so many women deficient in these nutrients?

We selected a group of women with serious premenstrual problems and, rather than use a single nutrient like B_6 or GLA, calculated their optimum nutritional requirements.[31] After all, since nutrients work together in the body and should be supplied together in the diet, to treat a condition with one nutrient alone is against all the principles of optimum nutrition.

Out of nine women we asked an independent doctor to select those with the most pronounced premenstrual problems. We then gave them the appropriate vitamin and mineral supplements. Each participant then recorded her tiredness, depression, bloatedness, tension, and headaches over the next four menstrual cycles.

The results clearly indicated that there was a substantial improvement for each premenstrual health problem of between 55 and 85 percent. Expressed as an average, a person on such a program could expect a 66 percent improvement in each of these premenstrual problems within three months. Here's what the doctor and participants said "before and after".

Subject 1

BEFORE

Doctor's report "She has had erratic periods since the age of 12. In 1978 she started progesterone therapy to relieve her premenstrual irrational outbursts, depression, lethargy, and bloatedness. It helped, but she still experienced depression, weepiness, bloatedness, and irrational behavior up to five days before her period."

Subject's report "Five days before my period I can't get up in the morning and my muscles feel weak. I put on weight, my eyes go puffy and I feel bloated. I also get very irritable and tense, and have difficulty sleeping. I always get headaches."

AFTER

Doctor's report "Improved considerably for one month, then relapsed, now improving again. More energy, head-

aches gone completely, sleep improved, less irritable."
Subject's report "Getting up is no longer a problem, I have much more energy. My bloatedness is better, depression is better, I'm much less irritable, I've had no headaches and sleep is no problem. I've noticed all symptoms occur later. In fact, my period is due in two days and I have no symptoms at all."

Subject 2
BEFORE
Doctor's report "Smokes 40 a day; coughs. Irregular periods before going on the pill in 1979. Symptoms of tension, nervousness, tearfulness, depression, and lack of energy, not exclusively before period."
Subject's report "I feel bloated and heavy two days before my period. I get depressed, tearful, and am very easily upset. I feel tense and my skin condition gets worse and I get more blemishes."

AFTER
Doctor's report "Significant improvement in all symptoms. Has not been warned of periods prior to their onset during this time."
Subject's report "Haven't noticed bloatedness at all. Indigestion and wind are much better. I don't get the tension, depression, and tears before my period. My skin is much better, it isn't dry and flaky like before, I have no dandruff, my thrush has gone, I've stopped losing hair, my nose is not so blocked, I don't get the prickly sensations in my legs due to my varicose veins, and I no longer get a coated tongue or cracked lips."

Subject 3
BEFORE
Doctor's report "Previous history is good. Experiences abdominal pain, depression, and irrational emotional outbursts, tension, listlessness, and some weight gain prior to period. Also sometimes headaches."
Subject's report "I experience tiredness and lethargy, both in body and mind, usually one day before period. I get

bloated, depressed, and tense four days before, and occasionally get a headache on the side of my head when waking."

AFTER
Doctor's report "Improvement in energy, no change in headaches."
Subject's report "I've had a definite improvement in energy, both in body and mind. Depression before my period is less noticeable, tension is a little less, there wasn't a lot of bloatedness, and headaches occur at the same time but I get them less frequently. I've noticed my skin is less dry, I've had fewer colds, my cracked lips are better and I haven't had a nosebleed."

These testimonials illustrate the results experienced by many women who have tried the nutritional approach to menstrual problems. With optimum nutrition there is no doubt that all aspects of life to do with the sexual cycle and fertility can be improved.

7

The Five-Factor Diet

Have you ever seen a fat fox? What is it about animals in a natural environment that keeps them the right size? Is it because they have just enough food to eat and no more? An unlikely theory.

The human animal is not so lucky. An estimated 70 percent of people in the United States are currently overweight. Your ideal weight depends upon your build, but we have become programed to accept being overweight as normal. For instance, I am 5ft 10in. I used to weigh 154lb. Now I weigh 143lb. I run ten to 20 miles a week and feel much stronger than I used to. But when I first lost weight my friends and relatives were most concerned! The best figures for "ideal weight" are the ones provided by life insurance companies; they know the facts about weight and longevity. Average figures are used too often. A 5ft 6in. women of medium build, for example, may weigh anything between 110lb and 126lb for maximum life expectancy.

Are we overweight because we eat too much? A plausible theory, but one that doesn't fit all the facts. Fat people actually eat *less* than thin people,[1] and, as a nation, our total food consumption is going down, but weight is not declining. Somehow counting calories just doesn't work.

Imagine that there are some natural laws, some balancing factors, that wild animals obey but we do not, that keeps their weight at the desired level. All we would have to do is obey these laws and our weight would also stabilize. I believe these laws are known, and with that knowledge comes the end to the long search for a way to achieve permanent weight loss. But first, let us look at the theories that don't work, and see what we can learn from them.

The Con Behind Calorie Counting

Almost all existing diets believe that what goes in, minus what goes out (in exercise), ends up as a wad of fat around your middle. Therefore the answer is to eat less and exercise more.

Armed with calorie charts and even calorie calculators, countless people perform mathematical equations over breakfast, lunch, and dinner. Calorie counting, the most popular approach to weight loss, is not without its difficulties and failures. We decided to test the practical usefulness of the approach by asking ten long-term overweight women to follow a 1,000 calorie diet, including high-fiber foods, for a period of three months. All women had been overweight for many years and were clearly committed to completing this diet. They were given diet-sheets and recipes. But six out of the ten gave up within three months and reverted to their usual eating habits.

Of the four who stuck to their diets as best as they could, one actually made a gain of 4lb, while one lost 15lbs! The third registered no change at all, and the fourth lost just 2lb. The average loss in weight over the four was 3lb 4oz. The one person who lost a substantial amount reveals a one in ten success rate, since ten people started the diet with good intentions.

Many dieters blame themselves for failure: "The diet works but I don't. I have no willpower. If only I had stuck to the diet better and for longer. Next time . . .", and the weight creeps back on. There is some truth in this; the support of slimming groups and the coercion of weight-loss clubs may increase that iron will we're meant to have. But what is the point of recommending a diet that few people can stick to?

A calorie is a unit of heat. Technically, it is the amount of heat needed to raise 1g of water by 1° centigrade. The dieter's calorie is actually a "kilo-calorie", a thousand calories. The calorie content in foods varies enormously. Fat is the most calorific substance, followed by carbohydrate, then protein. Different activities use up different amounts of calories. For example, an hour of walking uses up 200 calories, while half an hour of energetic cycling may use up 250 calories. If you eat more than you burn off in activity you get fat, and if you eat less than you burn off you get thin. Simple, isn't it?

But actually it isn't that simple. According to Dr. Colgan, some of the athletes he works with burn off over 7,000 calories, but eat only 3,500 calories. In theory they should have disappeared completely by now! An investigation of people living in famine conditions in the Warsaw ghetto during World War II showed the same contradiction.[2] With an average calorie intake of 700 to 800 calories per day and a daily requirement of, say, 2,500 calories, a deficit of 1,241,000 calories would build up over two years. The average body has 30lb of fat to dispose of, representing 100,000 calories at most. Even if all this fat were lost, what happens to the remaining million calories?

Since 1lb of fat is roughly equivalent to 4,000 calories, eating 40,000 fewer calories per year should mean losing 10lb in the first year, 49lb by the fifth year and over 98lb by the tenth year. After 15 years you would vanish entirely— all by eating one less apple every day! (One apple provides 100 calories a day or 36,500 a year.) Turn the equation round the other way, and the simple sin of an extra daily apple would mean a gain of 98lb every ten years.

The calorie equation for exercise is equally ridiculous. Cycle vigorously for 15 minutes each day and you will lose 10lb in the first year? Quite possibly. But 98lb after ten years? No chance. And remember, according to calorie theory, just one extra apple a day undoes all that hard work!

The problems with calorie theory are not just mathematical ones. Its proponents have realized that the major problem in calorie-controlled diets is that people get *hungry*. The question then became: "How can we eat only 1,000 calories a day *and* feel satisfied?" The answer was fiber.

The Fiber Fad

Within days of the publication of *The F-Plan Diet* by
Audrey Eyton (Bantam, 1984), fiber sales exploded. My
wife Liz, who runs a health food shop, was ordering bran
in 25kg sacks, and selling it faster than she could pack it in
bags. With the boom came high-fiber tablets and high-
fiber convenience foods, promoted as the slimmer's best
friend. This by-product of refined flour has been promoted
to a princely food, but partly for the wrong reason. Studies
using increased quantities of grain fiber do not consistently
report effects on weight. Now, a few years later, although
the fiber boom still continues, may have found that high-
fiber, low-calorie diets are not the magic answer they had
hoped for.

On page 64 I recorded the results of such a diet on four
women who stuck to it, taking a recommended 35g of fiber
per day. The results were not impressive. We then tested
high-fiber tablets without a calorie controlled diet. Again
we took ten overweight women and put them on two
common brands of fiber supplements in tablet form sold as
slimming aids. One brand contained 500mg of cereal fiber
per tablet; the other only 100mg, though each had the
same recommended dose: six tablets a day. This time, five
of the ten subjects dropped out. After three months, the
remaining five showed an average weight loss of only 1lb
9oz. The maximum loss was 7lb, next best was 4lb, two
subjects showed no change, and one put on 3lb.

Once again, these results are not very impressive, although high-fiber diets may help a small percentage of
people to lose weight. They are, however, definitely
recommended for many other health reasons: for instance,
it is well known that those on high-fiber diets have less
risk of bowel cancer,[3] diabetes,[4] diverticular disease[5], and
constipation.[6]

Fiber is a natural constituent of a healthy diet that is
high in fruits, vegetables, nuts, seeds, and grains. There is
no need to add extra bran to your diet if you eat these
foods already. Dr. Pfeiffer at the Brain Bio Center in New

Jersey has stressed the danger of adding bran to a nutrient-poor diet, since bran contains a high level of phytate, which reduces our absorption of some essential minerals, including zinc. Bran should not be recommended to those with a diet high in refined foods, without first ensuring adequate zinc status.

Fiber is calorie-free and there is little doubt that a diet high in fiber can be satisfying and easy to follow. A pound of carrots will fill you up a good deal more than two cookies. But while we have learned that low-calorie diets do help maintain correct weight and that high-fiber content in the diet makes this easier, there are many more pieces of the puzzle.

Keeping the Fire Burning

The problem with the theory that "food minus exercise equals fat" is that the ability to use and burn off fat varies from person to person. We all know friends whose appetites know no bounds, yet they stay slim, while we nibble at smaller and smaller servings in a desperate attempt to control our weight. It is known that fat people actually eat *less* than lean people in proportion to their weight and that lean people are more active. The increase in weight and decrease in calorie requirement that comes as people get older exemplifies this.

The process of turning food into energy is called "metabolism". The rate at which we burn our food is called the "metabolic rate". The faster your metabolic rate, the harder it is to put on weight. An athlete develops a fast metabolic rate—a fast-burning fire—and, providing the training continues, he or she will not get fat even if excess calories are eaten. On the other hand, deprive the body of food and the metabolic rate will drop. This explains why people half-starved in concentration camps during the war did not die, even though their calorie intake was far too low by "calorie theory". Their bodies adapted to the situation they were in.

Although crash diets are not intended as starvation, the human body, programed to survive, reacts exactly as if they were. While on such a diet, especially if it is substantially different from normal, the metabolic rate drops; the fire is turned down. So we become used to living off less. Like a walrus, we also become slower and feel less vital. When the ten-day diet is over, back come the calories and the weight, until we weigh even more than before, because our metabolic rate may not recover from the disruption. In this way, dieting can actually make you fat. This is well explained in Geoffrey Cannon's book, *Dieting Makes You Fat* (Simon & Schuster, 1985).

Despite these facts being well known, none of the popular slimming organizations makes use of the factors known to increase metabolic rate. Indeed, most assume that metabolic activity does not alter. All we can do, they say, is exercise more (which is not easy when overweight!) or eat less. But it is my belief that few people can achieve permanent weight loss *only* by reducing calorie intake, and that these few may have to resign themselves to a lifetime of carefully controlled eating. Consider again the analogy of the thin fox. Despite an abundant food supply, the fox stays thin. Could it be born with a self-regulating fat burner? If so, what's happened to ours?

Man is an animal that has evolved over millions of years into a precise and awe-inspiring machine. This machine and the basis of its existence, the cell, are essentially the same from mammal to mammal. Only in the relatively recent past have we developed extra delicate software, the cortical brain. With our intelligence, communication, and self-consciousness we have separated ourselves from other animals, but physiologically we are still very much the same. So what is different about the habits of man, the most domesticated animal, and of foxes?

Factor 1—The Vitality Diet

Most food in our natural environment comes with the full complement of nutrients needed to metabolize it. The efficiency of our metabolism depends not only on the quantity of food but also its quality, meaning the balance of at least 28 different vitamins and minerals. By refining food mankind has cheated himself. Food was fine before, but now the concentrated sweetness of sugar can be eaten without the rest of the fruit, the fullness of fat can satisfy our appetites without the rest of the nut or seed. Two-thirds of the average western diet consists of refined—or, more accurately, dismembered—nutrient-poor foods. These foods upset our metabolic rate and, as it drops, we need less food to maintain the same weight. By following the vitality diet (Chapter 10) we can get back in line with nature.

Allergy or Addiction?

Allergy is a word that frequently conjures up meaning beyond its original intention. Allergies are simply altered reactions to certain substances, and most of us have them. A common one is hay fever, which is a reaction to pollen. Reactions to certain food groups are equally common. Food allergies are often the result of over-eating in a certain food group, so it is not surprising that people are often allergic to the very food they would find hardest to give up. It can be like an addiction—we can literally be addicted to the food that does us most harm. When this food is removed from the diet, symptoms will get worse before they get better, as with any withdrawal from addiction. The most common "allegens" (foods that cause allergies) are:

WHEAT	YEAST
MILK	ALCOHOL
SUGAR	FOOD ADDITIVES
CORN	

An allergy to any one of these can substantially increase weight, often through the retention of excess fluid. Some of my clients have lost up to 7lb in fluid as a result of avoiding their allergen. If you suspect you are allergic, make a list of all the foods you suspect and all the foods and drinks you would have difficulty giving up. Avoid these entirely for at least 20 days and see what happens. If there is any change in your health or weight it would be advisable for you to see a nutritionist who can help you pinpoint the substances to which you react.

Factor 2—The Vitamin Factor

Our bodies crave nutrients. The trouble is lack of communication. We don't hear, "Give me vitamin B_6", we hear, "Give me more food!" So we eat more vitamin-deficient food and the hunger goes on. Sugar is a good example of this. When we refine and denutrientize sugar, our bodies cannot handle it and gradually become increasingly unable to tolerate it. Diabetes or hypoglycemia can ensue, and so can excess weight, because intolerance to sugar slows the rate of metabolism. Give the body enough nutrients, on the other hand, and everything will be burned off more efficiently. The most important will be the vitamin B Complex, especially B_3 and B_6, vitamin C, and the minerals zinc and chromium. These regulate our energy production and blood sugar levels and assist in digestion. B_6 and zinc also help regulate sex and adrenal hormones, thereby stabilizing our emotional moods.

I used to treat overweight people with extra vitamin supplements alone with a success rate of around 40 percent. With the five-factor diet I believe 90 percent of people will be guaranteed to lose weight. See Chapter 9 for your special vitamin needs for weight loss.

Factor 3—Glucomannan Fiber

The high-fiber approach to weight loss has a number of good points. First, a shift to high-fiber foods—basically wholegrains, fruit, and raw vegetables—is a shift to a healthier, more nutritious diet. It protects against disease and is also more filling. Two bars of chocolate contain the same number of calories as 5lb of carrots—but the carrots would fill you up far more effectively!

There are many different forms of fiber, which have different effects on weight loss. One of these is Glucomannan. Unlike many fibers, which make up the outside shell of plant cells, Glucomannan is found inside the plant cell of the Japanese Konjac plant. Konjac (whose Latin name, *Amorphophallus*, will give you some idea of what it looks like!) has been grown and used in food for years by the Japanese. My attention was drawn to this unusual fiber by two studies that reported astounding weight loss with only 3g of Glucomannan per day. (Most diets recommend at least 35g of fiber per day for any effect.) One researcher in California gave 12 obese people 3g of Glucomannan per day and found an average weight loss of 9lb 11oz.[7] Another in North Dakota repeated this study over a four-week period and found a 5lb 5oz loss.[8]

These stories sounded too good to be true. Slim without suffering! Just take a few pills each day and the pounds will drop off you *and* you will become healthier, because Glucomannan has some very beneficial side effects. It decreases the diabetic's need for insulin,[9] it lowers the levels of triglycerides in the blood, which are associated with heart disease,[10] and is a very effective cure for constipation.[11]

We decided to test this "wonderfiber" for ourselves. We selected 40 obese women and assigned them to one of four groups. Group A received placebos (dummy tablets); group B received tablets containing 500mg of pure Glucomannan; group C received two well-known brands of slimming tablets based on ordinary grain fiber; group D were put on a controlled diet of 1,000 calories and placebos. To make sure the test was fair, we matched the groups for average weight, which was 170lb. The experimenter who interviewed the participants was instructed to read out a speech explaining when and how to take the tablets. All the participants received the same speech and neither they nor the experimenter knew that placebos and different forms of fiber were being used as well as Glucomannan. Three months later we analyzed the results.[12]

Not only did those on Glucomannan lose a substantial amount of weight without any alteration to diet and exercise, but their weight loss was significantly better than those following a calorie-controlled diet or taking other high-fiber tablets. Those on the placebos lost no weight,

so we knew that the Glucomannan effect was real. One
participant lost 16lb and another 13lb; the worst results
were gains in weight, but these were only of 2lb for two
of the women. The average weight loss for those on
Glucomannan was 6lb 5½oz.

The surprising results of Glucomannan alone illustrated
to us just how different fiber can be. Since Glucomannan
swells to 100 times its original volume when placed in
liquid, we wondered whether its effect on weight loss was
due to a decrease in appetite caused by swelling in the
stomach. Wheat bran, which only swells to three times its
volume, may have been ineffective for this purpose. However, only two out of nine women on Glucomannan experienced any suppression or reduction of appetite. In the
placebo group, one out of three did, and in the group
taking other high-fiber tablets one out of five did. Although Glucomannan may suppress the appetite slightly, it
is unlikely that this is the only reason for its success,
although it does prevent extreme overeating and could
therefore be useful to those who "binge".

How to Take Glucomannan Fiber
Unlike other forms of dietary fiber, 3g of Glucomannan per
day is enough to induce weight loss as well as stabilize
blood sugar levels and lower cholesterol levels. Since 3g is
approximately a tablespoon of powder, it can be taken in
capsule form or made into a gel with water. Either way, it
should always be taken with a large glasss of water, as it is
extremely absorbent. It is best taken 30 minutes before
eating in order to obtain the maximum reduction in appetite.

Glucomannan fiber usually comes in 500mg capsules,
therefore six tablets must be taken each day. If you eat
three major meals a day, it is best to take more Glucomannan
the larger the meal. For example, take one capsule before
breakfast, two before lunch, and three before dinner.
Some people have experienced a slight feeling of bloatedness
and an increase in intestinal wind for up to seven days
after starting on Glucomannan. These are the only side-
effects and they disappear completely within a week.

Factor 4—Conscious Eating

The first thing you ever did was eat; within minutes of being born each infant receives its first sustenance from its mother. But suckling provides far more than food. In a famous experiment, infant monkeys were presented with the choice of two surrogate mothers—constructed dummies complete with teats. One provided milk, but had no fur, the other gave no milk but did give the tactile experience of fur. The baby monkeys chose the tactile sensation rather than the food.[13]

For baby humans the tactile sense and security of the breast is soon associated with food. As well as providing nourishment, eating is emotive: later in life, it can become associated with pleasing, rebelling, imitating, rewarding, even punishing. Examples are the girl who eats sparingly, like her mother, because she also wants to be thin; the boy who eats only certain foods because they make him "big and strong"; the rebellion against "eat it up or you won't get any dessert"; the reward of sweets if you do something good. By adolescence a multitude of mental factors govern when, how, what, and how much we eat.

"Five hundred people were asked what they fear most in the world and 190 answered that their greatest fear is 'getting fat'" (Kim Chernin, *The Obsession*, Harper & Row, 1981). The fear of fat, the love and hatred of food is a real social problem of epidemic proportions. With the fear has come a rapid rise in maladaptive eating behavior: compulsive eating, crash dieting, bulimia (weight control by vomiting), and anorexia nervosa. At least 95 percent of sufferers are women and there is little doubt that social pressures play a significant part. Torn between the advertising images of the sexually "perfect" woman and perpetual sensory bombardment with tantalizing foods, between the image of the thin and sensuous woman designed to attract her man, and the caring, providing "earth mother" image, twentieth-century woman must be all things to all people. For twentieth-century man, being overweight is of relatively less significance: a glance at our politicians, trade union leaders, and executives may even suggest that for men success and power are equated with excess weight!

Brought to light by Susie Orbach in *Fat is a Feminist Issue* (Berkley, 1984), the psychological role that fat plays in our society is a vital issue for anybody who intends to maintain the right weight. To help my clients, we developed a series of simple exercises to help people explore the psychological side of eating. They are divided into the three A's:

AWARENESS is the first: awareness of when, how, and what you eat; your beliefs, facts and fantasies about eating and about being thin or fat.

ACCEPTANCE is the opposite to resistance. So often we are taught that the only way to win is to fight, and certainly there are those who lose weight through sheer willpower. However, by understanding that all past and present eating habits are just an attempt to compensate for something, to find pleasure or security, it is possible to eat (and on occasions overeat) without guilt or remorse. To accept your habits is not to give in—it's a step nearer of being in control of your eating behavior.

ACTION can only really be effective when we know completely what it is we are reacting to. So often when we want to eat it is not because we are hungry, but as a way to cope with frustration, boredom, or too much pressure. Once the motive is fully understood, we can choose other, less fattening options to dissipate these feelings more effectively.

Factor 5—Exercise

Regular aerobic exercise like swimming, running, cycling, and aerobics are a vital part of maintaining your ideal weight. Although it burns few calories directly, the effects of 15 minutes' exercise each day can substantially raise the metabolic rate.[14] Whatever exercise program you start it must become an integral part of your life and daily routine (see Chapter 11).

These observations form the theory behind the five-factor diet. With each factor you will find there are many side-effects—such as increased memory, alertness, fitness, and happiness and fewer minor ailments like colds and infections. You won't have to starve yourself, nor will you have to plunge into mammoth exercise routines. What you will have to do is this:

1. Follow the VITALITY DIET
2. Work out your PERSONAL HEALTH PROGRAM
3. Take GLUCOMANNAN fiber for the first three months
4. Do the CONSCIOUS EATING exercises
5. Do the BLISSS EXERCISES every day (see Chapter 11)

Who says losing weight can't be fun?

8

The Pollution Solution

Researchers at the California Institute of Technology have been studying the changes in lead concentrations throughout the world—in ocean beds, Greenland snows, and soil samples. Their work[1] shows us that lead concentration, even in unpolluted Greenland, has risen between 500 and 1,000 times since prehistoric ages. Most of this increase has taken place in the last 100 years, and is mainly a result of industrial pollution and the exhaust from cars. Comparison of lead found in humans showed a similar 500- to 1000-fold increase.[2] How can we be sure that we are not poisoning ourselves with such large levels of lead? We cannot.

Of course, the first questions we must ask are: what are the effects of lead, and how much is too much? Guidelines put out in different countries vary quite considerably. In the USA the maximum level is 40mcg/dl regardless of sex. A much-criticized government report published in the UK in 1980 recommended 35mcg/dl as the maximum safe level for lead measured in blood.[3] Professor Bryce-Smith, world authority on lead toxicity, considers that even this is too high. He advocates 20mcg/dl as the absolute maximum safe level with proper medical supervision for adults, but for children, he says, this is still too high. His recommendations are further confirmed by three recent research studies that have all shown conclusively that levels of lead as low as 13mcg/dl affect the behavior of children and lower their intelligence. When we consider that the *average* lead level in the USA is 9mcg/dl we must come to the conclusion that lead may be damaging the minds of a substantial number of our children. Let's examine the evidence.

The Needleman Study

The first study to shake the status quo regarding lead toxicity was carried out by Herbert Needleman, an associate professor of child psychiatry, who looked at a group of 2,146 children in 1st and 2nd grade schools in Birmingham, Alabama.[4] He examined lead concentrations in discarded milk teeth to obtain information on more long-term lead levels than that given by simple blood tests. He then asked the children's schoolteachers to rate their behavior using a questionnaire designed to measure a number of characteristics, such as ability to concentrate, tendency to daydream, etc. He also ran a series of behavioral, intellectual, and physiological tests on each child, before dividing the children into six groups according to the lead concentration shown in their teeth.

Needleman's results showed a clear relationship between high concentrations and poor behavior, as rated by the teachers without knowledge of the children's lead levels. He also found the average IQ for the high-lead children was 4.5 points lower than that of the low-lead group. Reaction times, which are a measure of attentiveness, were consistently worse in those with higher lead levels. Even EEG (electroencephalograph) readings, which measure brain-wave patterns, showed clear differences related to lead concentration. Perhaps the most interesting result was that none of the high-lead children had an IQ above 125 points, whereas in the low-lead group five percent did. Professor Needleman concluded: "The question of whether low level lead exposure is associated with significant brain alterations no longer needs—or deserves—prolonged and debilitating debate. Action on lead, clearly warranted, long delayed, and easily obtained, could be the first in a series of steps to protect the legacy we owe our children—a world in which the physical and social arrangements we proved permit their brains and futures to achieve their full reach."

Although Needleman's study shows us that the behavior and intelligence of normal children are clearly affected by lead, we cannot determine safe levels for lead concentration in blood, since his study used teeth. The amount of lead in teeth identifies the need for more long-term measures, but it is not the most practical method for screening purposes: a screening program based on yanking out our teeth could hardly be considered progress!

The Lansdown Study

Richard Lansdown and William Yule, psychologists at the University of London, decided to repeat Needleman's study on London children using levels of lead in blood instead of in teeth. The children selected had an average blood level of 13.52mcg/dl (remember that 35mcg/dl is the "safe" level), which is similar to the average found in other national studies of lead levels. Again the children's behavior was rated by their teachers, and their IQ was measured.

Lansdown's results were even more striking than Needleman's.[5] The difference in IQ score between high- and low-lead children was seven IQ points, even though none of the children had lead levels above the so-called "safe" level. Figure 4 shows the children's behavior as rated by their teachers. The children with high levels of lead had far worse behavior ratings and their IQs were also seven points below average.

A further study by Gerhard Winneke, Director of the Medical Institute of Environmental Hygiene in Düsseldorf in West Germany, found essentially the same results.[6] He studied 458 children with an average blood lead level of 14.3mcg/dl, and found a difference in IQ of five to seven points between those with high and low lead levels. He also looked at the levels of lead in teeth and found that they were closely correlated to those in blood—a further confirmation of Needleman's results.

Are You at Risk?

Although adults are by no means safe from the dangers of lead poisoning it is children who are most at risk, especially up to the age of 12 when high lead can cause irreversi-

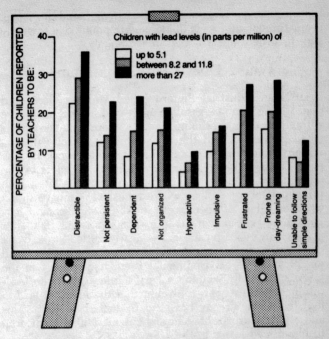

Figure 4 Performance of children with different levels of lead

ble brain damage. Children absorb lead more easily than adults and are frequently exposed to high concentrations in dust. This means that a high proportion of children, particularly in cities, are absorbing enough lead to affect their intellectual development. The most common symptoms of lead toxicity are inability to concentrate, disturbed sleep, uncharacteristic outbursts of aggression, fussiness about food, sinus conditions, and headaches. Children under eight are most at risk, although it is only the size of the problem that diminishes from age eight—it doesn't disappear altogether. Adults suffering from lead poisoning are likely to experience chronic lack of physical and mental energy, headaches, depression, and loss of memory. According to a report by the Federal Register in 1978, lead exposure leads to kidney failure, high blood pressure, premature aging, loss of libido, and impotence in the male and disturbed menstruation in the female.[7]

Where Does Lead Come From?

In 1921 an industrial chemist called Midgley discovered that adding lead to gasoline increased its octane rating without additional refining, thereby increasing the profits of oil companies and the lead industry. Despite deaths, insanity, and illness among 139 poisoned workers, the profits from adding lead to gas were put into effect by the oil industry throughout the world. Sixty years later, with the effects of excess lead well established, we have to ask whether it has all been worth it. The USSR thought not, and banned the use of gas in its major cities in 1960 after research in 1958. Japan's gas is nearly all lead-free. West Germany now enforces the lowest European levels of lead in gas, and the Environmental Protection Agency in the USA is gradually winning a legal battle against the lead-producing industry, to control further the levels of lead in fuel that have already been cut by half since 1976. This and other measures have brought about a 30 percent drop in blood lead levels in the USA.[8]

The Politics of Lead

The claim that cars perform better on leaded fuel appears to be a myth, according to a report by the Environmental Protection Agency in the USA.[8] This report also concludes that the extra cost of more refined 2-star fuel is zero, and that more refined 4-star may cost only 2.2 cents more per US gallon. They conclude that totally banning lead from gasoline would actually save money, due to decreased maintenance costs and engine wear in cars.

There are alternatives to lead octane-improvers, which are used by many countries, including the USA, USSR, Japan, and West Germany. The issue comes down to money versus health, and only increased public pressure will produce a sensible solution—a total ban on lead in gasoline. Already the reduction of lead pollution from unleaded gasoline has brought about a 30 percent drop in blood lead level.[9]

Lead from Gasoline

The usual assumption is that lead comes directly from inhalation of airborne lead from car exhausts, but this may not always be the major source. A considerable quantity of lead from cars and buses ends up on the food we eat. Whether it comes through milk produced by the cow that eats the grass by the roadside,[10] or directly from vegetables, the result is too much lead in our foods. Figure 5,

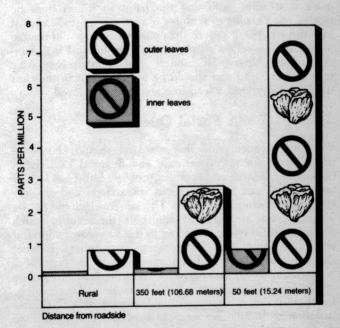

Figure 5 Lead levels found in cabbages grown at various distances from motor traffic.

based on research by the Reading Environmental Health Department, shows just how much lead can end up in our dinner. These levels may be further elevated when the grocer displays his foods both to us and to the traffic passing by his shop. Most scientists agree that at least 90 percent of the lead in food is due to fallout from car exhausts.

Other sources of lead include water, paint, and canned foods. Most pre-1940 houses have some lead piping, which causes a particular problem for those areas with soft water. However, a greater problem is the solder still used in plumbing which, if it is not properly done, leaches out into the water. People stripping old paint in houses for redecoration run a risk—it is best to remove such paint by using a steamer, softening the paint so it can then be peeled off. Burning or scraping old paint releases lead dust into the air. There's more than one reason to avoid double yellow lines—yellow paint contains the highest lead concentration! Almost all canned foods contain excessive quantities of lead and should be avoided. But in the cans used for baby food a lead-free solder is employed.

A Social Question

It seems inconceivable that mankind should choose to poison itself for industrial ease and financial gain. Lead poisoning is a large and complex problem but it has largely been unraveled. No longer can researchers and governments hide behind ignorance. The safe level should not be 35mcg/dl, nor should it be 12mcg/dl (the level at which there was little effect according to the Lansdown study): it should be half of this—5mcg/dl, say, or even less. Even at blood levels of 5mcg/dl, brain-wave patterns are disturbed. Nor should we be talking about reducing lead in gasoline and in processed foods: we should be banning it completely. Lead poisoning is clearly a social, political, and nutritional question with only one sensible answer. But what can we do to protect ourselves now?

Fortunately, a number of natural substances are known to help "chelate" toxic minerals—remove them from our bodies—and keep us healthy.

CALCIUM is effective at keeping down our lead levels.[11, 12] Keeping our calcium levels topped up makes it less easy for lead to be stored in our bones. Calcium is also particularly effective at keeping down cadmium and aluminium levels. Dolomite and bonemeal—a natural calcium supplement—may contain lead as well, so some researchers recommend other forms of calcium or magnesium supplements such as calcium and magnesium carbonate.

VITAMIN C is an all-rounder too.[13, 14] It has the ability to latch on to heavy metals in the blood and escort them out, sacrificing itself in the process. So high metal burdens call for more vitamin C. It is effective at removing lead, arsenic, and cadmium and is a most important part of any detoxification program.

PHOSPHORUS is another mineral that can help prevent the ravages of lead.[15] At a conference on lead and health, Professor Bryce-Smith said: "Dietary manipulation and the provision of a calcium and phosphate supplement may both be helpful."

ZINC has been shown to be good at reducing body levels of lead and cadmium.[16] A study by the Brain Bio Center achieved a 25 percent drop in lead levels over 24 weeks. Most of us could in any case benefit from extra zinc.

PECTIN is derived from apples; bananas, carrots, and citrus fruits are also excellent sources. It "chelates" heavy metals in the same way as alginic acid—one more reason for an apple a day.

SELENIUM is a mercury antagonist[17] and normally protects us from the mercury present in most seafood. Supplements are always a good idea if there are signs of excess mercury in the body. Selenium also acts similarly on arsenic and cadmium, although the effect is not so pronounced.

SULPHUR-containing AMINO ACIDS are found as the proteins in garlic, onions, and eggs. The specific amino acids, methionine and cystine, protect against mercury, cadmium, and lead toxicity.

Vitamin Vitality

Multinutrients Detoxify Best

Very little work has been done on the cumulative effects of using all the above natural detoxifiers together. Separately, good results have been achieved with vitamin C, zinc, and calcium in controlled experiments; the remainder have been clinically tested. Dr. Michael Colgan was the first to use a mulitnutrient formula as a means for lowering levels of toxic metals. He studied 16 children with learning and behavior and reading age (see Figure 3, p. 26). Dr. Colgan programs for them based on a number of factors including diet, symptoms, and a hair mineral analysis. All the children were put on a reading course and a behavior-modification course, but only some of them were given multinutrients.

Hair levels for the toxic metals were taken at week 1 and 21 in this 22-week study. Reading age, results on tests, IQ, and behavior-ratings by teachers and parents were monitored throughout the study. The children on supplements had a dramatic improvement in intelligence, behavior and reading age (see Figure 3, p. 26). Dr. Colgan stated in a recent conference[18] that the factor he thought most likely to be responsible for the increase was lowering of lead and cadmium levels. The average hair lead level before the study was around 30 parts per million (ppm), which decreased to 16ppm after 22 weeks. That's almost a 50 percent reduction in lead levels. The safe level given for lead in the hair is around 5ppm, although many children have levels far higher than this.

Research at my own institute using a multinutrient formula containing zinc, vitamin C, calcium phosphate, alginic acid, and pectin has shown consistent 50 percent reductions in lead levels. But the only real answer to the problem of lead and other environmental poisons is to ban their use in forms and for purposes where they are likely to end up in us.

9

Your Personal Health Program

How healthy do you want to be? If you want to realize your full potential, mentally and physically, finding out your optimum nutritional requirements is essential. But if your needs are unique, how do you find these out? Since 1980 I have been developing a simple system for analyzing people's nutrient needs, based on assessing the major factors that influence the individual's requirements. The account I give here is a simplification since the system is based on questions and answers, but it provides a useful assessment of what you need for optimum health. Nearly 2,000 people have benefited so far from this program, so I know what sort of results to expect. They include greater mental alertness, improved memory, more physical energy, better weight control, and a lowering of the risk of degenerative disease. Although many people with diagnosed illnesses have been helped while on a personal health program, it is not designed to treat illness so much as to prevent it. The claims made for "curing" advanced degenerative diseases with nutrition are often exaggerated: if you suffer from a recognized medical condition, please check that this program is compatible with any treatment you may already be receiving.

At least eight factors affect your optimum nutritional requirements. Factors such as your age, sex, and amount of exercise are easy to assess. But the effects of pollution, your past health history, and, of course, the nutrients (and antinutrients) supplied in your diet are not so straightforward to work out. But all these factors and more must be taken into account. There are three basic ways to go about it.

Diet Analysis

Diet may seem the obvious place to start. By finding out what goes in, one could know what is missing. But unfortunately, a breakdown of foods eaten over, say, a week, cannot take into account the variations in nutrient content in the food, your individual needs, nor how well the nutrient is used when, and if, it is absorbed. Last year in my clinic I saw at least 100 people who had superficially "perfect" diets, but still showed signs of vitamin deficiency. For many of these people the problem was poor absorption. These variables make some diet analyses done on a computer less than accurate.

Where diet analysis is useful is in assessing foods that are known to affect our nutrient needs—such as sugar, salt, coffee, tea, alcohol, food additives, and preservatives. Other factors, such as intake of fats, carbohydrates, protein, and calories, can also be determined from an analysis of your diet.

Biochemical Tests

Biochemical tests such as hair mineral analysis or vitamin blood tests give indisputable information about biochemical status. But not all of these tests provide useful information to help you build up your nutrition program. Any vitamin or mineral test, to be accurate, must reflect the ability of the nutrient to function in the body. For example, iron is a vital constituent of red blood cells; it helps to carry oxygen throughout the body. By measuring the iron status in your cells it is possible to get a good measure of your iron needs. On the other hand, vitamin B_6 has no function to perform in the blood—it is used in other chemical reactions, for example the production of the brain chemical serotonin, which helps us go to sleep. So a measure of the B_6 level in your blood would tell you nothing. In fact, if B_6 isn't being used properly in other parts of the body, blood levels may be high, although a state of deficiency exists elsewhere. So for vitamin B_6 a clever test has been devised, called a "functional enzyme test". Tryptophan, a constituent of protein, is acted upon by enzymes, which turn it into niacin (vitamin B_3) in the body. One of these enzymes is dependent on vitamin B_6. So if you do not have enough B_6, instead of making B_3 you produce a by-product, xanthurenic acid, which is excreted in the urine. By measuring the amount of xanthurenic acid excreted, it is possible to gauge whether you are getting enough B_6 and if it is being used properly.

Which Test Is Best?

Because each nutrient has a different function in the body, we cannot say that blood tests are better than urine tests, or that hair mineral levels provide more accurate information than blood levels. For each nutrient there are different tests depending on what we want to find out. For instance, there are over a dozen tests for zinc deficiency, depending on what zinc-dependent enzyme we want to test. These involve blood, urine, hair, sweat, and even a taste test.

To make an extensive series of tests would be expensive. My number one "value for money" test is hair mineral analysis, which tells you about mineral status. From a small sample of hair the levels of lead, cadmium, arsenic, aluminium, copper, and mercury can be tested: all of these are toxic in excess. Hair mineral analysis also provides useful information about calcium, magnesium, sodium, potassium, zinc, chromium, selenium, and manganese, although these results need careful interpretation. Hair mineral analysis can sometimes pinpoint problems of absorption, risk of heart disease, and other degenerative diseases.

To find out vitamin status, I use a series of "functional enzyme tests", which are more expensive than hair mineral analysis. However, the results of these enzyme tests usually confirm findings already made from deficiency symptom analysis. They are thus really necessary only for "fine-tuning" or when there is some doubt about the results of a previous test.

Deficiency symptom analysis is the most underestimated method of working out nutritional needs. It is based on over 200 signs and symptoms that have been found in cases of slight vitamin or mineral deficiency. For example, poor dream recall is related to B_6 deficiency, poor night vision to vitamin A deficiency. For many of these symptoms, the mechanism is understood. For example, vitamin A helps rhodopsin, the light-sensitive pigment needed to see in the dark. Symptoms such as poor night vision should not be seen as "vitamin deficiency diseases", but rather as early warning signs to show us that our bodies are not working perfectly. A small deficiency in vitamins C, B_3, or B_5 would all be shown in reduced energy because they are involved in the production of energy. But being low in energy doesn't necessarily mean you're B_3 deficient. After all, it could always be just because you're working too hard or sleeping badly. However, if you have five different symptoms, all associated with B_3 deficiency, then you are much more likely to be needing more vitamin B_3 to reach optimum health.

The advantage of deficiency symptom analysis is that health is being measured directly. Results are not dependent on whether you eat oranges that are high in vitamin C, or whether you absorb or utilize food well, as dietary analysis is. Some people have criticized this method because it relies on subjective information from the person concerned. Yet the large majority of medical diagnoses are in fact based on subjective information from the patient. If you want to find out how someone feels, isn't it obvious to ask? I always ask my clients why *they* think they're ill. Quite often they're right.

Your Personal Health Program

Underline each symptom that you suffer from often, and answer yes or no to each question. For each underlined symptom or yes answer, score one point. Put your score for each vitamin or mineral in the right-hand column.

Vitamin Profile

VITAMIN A   YOUR SCORE
Poor night vision; poor sense of smell; blemishes;
dry, flaky skin; dandruff; mouth ulcers; thrush;
cystitis; fatigue; loss of appetite, diarrhea; nausea.

Do you get more than three colds a year?
Do you smoke more than five cigarettes a week?   _____

VITAMIN D
Rheumatism; rickets; backache; lack of energy;
muscle cramps; tooth decay; hair loss; coarse
hair; dry skin; nearsightedness, chilblains.

Do you have pain and stiffness in the joints?
Do you have difficulty losing weight?   _____

VITAMIN E
Loss of sex drive; dry skin; excess sweating;
exhaustion after gentle exercise, easy bruising;
infertility; slow wound healing; varicose veins;
edema; puffy ankles.

Do you get cramps during or after a long walk?
Do cuts take a long time to stop bleeding?
Do you get out of breath easily?   _____

VITAMIN C
Colds; lack of energy; infections; allergies;
wrinkles; sagging skin; poor lactation; bad
digestion; bleeding gums; dental cavities, easy
bruising; nosebleeds; slow wound healing,
anemia.

Do you smoke more than five cigarettes a week?
Do you live in a heavy traffic area?
Is your life-style very stressful?   _____

VITAMIN B COMPLEX

Confusion; irritability; depression; hair loss; premature grey hair; bad skin; poor appetite; insomnia; difficulty relaxing; constipation; sleepiness after meals; allergies; hay fever; poor memory.

Do you wake up tired?
Do you run out of energy easily?
Do you feel tense?   _____

VITAMIN B_1

Tender muscles; stomach pains; constipation; prickly sensations in the legs; eye pains.

Do you have difficulty making decisions?
Are you losing weight?
Do you have difficulty breathing?   _____

VITAMIN B_2

Bloodshot, itchy eyes; burning or "gritty" eyes; sore tongue; cracked lips; cataracts; eczema; dull, oily hair; split nails; trembling; sluggishness; dizziness.

Are you sensitive to light?   _____

VITAMIN B_3

Fatigue; acne; headaches; loss of appetite; migraines; bad breath; skin eruptions; insomnia; irritability; tender gums; depression; rough, inflamed skin; tremors; allergies; loss of memory; coated tongue.

Do you swing from being hyperactive and overexcited to being very depressed?
Are you often anxious and fearful?   _____

VITAMIN B5
Apathy; abdominal pains; restlessness; vomiting;
asthma; allergies; burning feet; muscle cramps;
exhaustion.

Do you find it hard to concentrate?   _____

VITAMIN B6
Irritability; water retention; bloatedness;
depression; loss of hair; cracks around mouth
and eyes; numbness; muscle cramps; slow
learning; pregnancy sickness or depression;
allergies; nervousness; tingling hands;
menopausal arthritis.

Do you have difficulty recalling your dreams?
Are you taking the birth control pill?   _____

Mineral Profile
CALCIUM AND MAGNESIUM
Tooth decay; muscle cramps; brittle fingernails;
arthritis; nervousness; insomnia; depression;
muscle tremors; irritability.   _____

IRON
Anemia; pale skin; difficulty breathing; sore
tongue; fatigue; weakness.   _____

ZINC
Stretch marks; white marks under nails; poor
eyesight; poor sense of taste and smell; slow
wound healing; slow hair growth; slow growth
in children; hair loss; acne.   _____

MANGANESE
Lack of energy; lack of sex drive; arthritis;
dizziness; fits; knee problems.   _____

SELENIUM
Premature aging; poor resistance to infection;
high blood pressure; history of cancer; history of
cardiovascular disease; cataracts; arthritis.   _____

CHROMIUM
Need for frequent meals; difficulty digesting fats;
slow growth; headaches; excessive sleepiness;
dizziness or irritability after six hours without
food.   _____

Stress Check
Do you feel guilty when relaxing?
Do you have a persistent need for recognition or
achievement?
Are you unclear about your goals in life?
Are you especially competitive?
Do you work harder than most?
Do you easily become angry?
Do you often do two or three tasks
simultaneously?
Do you become impatient if people or things hold
you up?
Do you find it difficult to admit openly to failure
or defeat?   _____

If you answer yes more than four times, add two points to
your ratings for vitamins B_1, B_2, B_3, B_5, B_6, and C. If you
answer yes more than six times, add three points to your
ratings for these vitamins.

Exercise Check
Do you take exercise that noticeably raises your
heartbeat for at least 20 minutes more than three
times a week?
Does your job involve lots of walking, lifting, or
any other vigorous activity?
Do you regularly play a sport? (tennis, softball,
etc.)

Do you have any physically tiring hobbies?
(gardening, carpentry, etc.)
Are you in serious training for an athletic event?
Do you consider yourself fit?   _____

All the above activities increase your need for certain
nutrients. If you answer yes more than twice, add one
point to your ratings for vitamin B Complex, C, and E. If
you answer yes more than three times, add two points to
your ratings for these vitamins.

Pollution Check
Do you live in a city or by a busy road?
Do you smoke more than five cigarettes a day?
Do you spend more than two hours a week in
heavy traffic?
Do you exercise (jog, cycle, play sports) by
busy roads?
Do you eat canned foods more than five times a
week?
Do you buy foods exposed to exhaust fumes from
busy roads?
If your house has lead water pipes, do you drink
tap water? (pre-1940 houses, especially in cities,
usually do)
Do you drink more than 1 oz of alcohol a day?
(one glass of wine, 1 pint of beer, or one
measure of spirits)
Do you suffer from headaches?
Do you frequently feel tired?
Are you sometimes hyperactive or do you have
difficulty sleeping?   _____

If you answer yes more than four times, add two points to
your ratings for vitamin C, calcium, and zinc (also add
200mg of pectin to your nutritional program). If you
answer yes more than six times, add four points to your
ratings for these nutrients.

Heart Check
Is your blood pressure above 140/90?
Is your pulse after 15 minutes' rest above 75?
Are you more than 14lb over your ideal weight?
Do you smoke more than five cigarettes a day?
Do you do less than two hours of vigorous
exercise (one hour if you are over 50) a week?
Do you eat more than one tablespoonful of sugar
each day?
Is your life-style stressful?
Do you often have headaches?
Do you feel tired and sluggish most of the time?
Do you eat meat more than five times a week?   _____

If you answer yes more than four times, add one point to
your ratings for vitamins C, B_3, E, and selenium. If you
answer yes more than six times, add two points to your
ratings for these nutrients. If you have high blood pressure, limit your intake of vitamin E to 200 IU per day for
the first month, then 400 IU per day. Do not take more
than 400 IU without consulting your doctor.

Adjusting for Age
Special requirements exist for children and older people.
Scores and final nutrient requirements should be adjusted
as follows for those under 14 or over 50 years old.

YOUNGER THAN 3 Take 25 percent of the final nutrient
requirements, except for calcium, magnesium, zinc, and
pectin (50 percent).

AGES 3 TO 6 Take 50 percent of the final nutrient requirements, except for calcium, magnesium, zinc, and pectin
(75 percent).

AGES 6 TO 12 Take 65 percent of the final nutrient requirements, except for calcium, magnesium, zinc, and pectin
(full dose).

AGES 12 TO 14 Take 75 percent of the final nutrient
requirements, except for calcium, magnesium, zinc, and
pectin (full dose).

CHILDREN'S RULE OF THUMB
If in doubt about vitamin doses for children simple divide an adult's requirements by weight. For example, a 70lb child would have half the requirement of a fully-grown man.

OVER 50
Ensure you are supplementing your diet every day with at least 300mg of calcium, 150mg of magnesium, and 40mcg of chromium.

How to Work Out Your Optimum Vitamin and Mineral Levels

From the vitamin and mineral profiles you will have arrived at your score. This should then be adjusted depending on your score for the stress, exercise, pollution, and heart checks and finally depending on your age. Now, using the vitamin and mineral level charts on pp. 95 and 96, you'll be able to work out your ideal level for each vitamin and mineral.

Vitamin	Unit	Score				Your ideal level
		0–4	5–6	7–8	9 or more	
A (Retinol)	IU	7,500	10,000	15,000	20,000	_____
D	IU	400	600	800	1,000	_____
E	IU	100	300	500	1,000	_____
C	mg	1,000	2,000	3,000	4,000	_____
B_1 (Thiamine)	mg	25	50	75	100	_____
B_2 (Riboflavin)	mg	25	50	75	100	_____
B_3 (Niacin)	mg	50	75	100	150	_____
B_5 (Pantothenic acid)	mg	50	100	200	300	_____
B_6 (Pyridoxine)	mg	50	100	200	250	_____
B_{12}	mcg	5	10	50	100	_____
Folic acid	mcg	50	100	200	400	_____
Biotin	mcg	50	100	150	200	_____
Choline	mg	25	50	100	150	_____
Inositol	mg	25	50	100	150	_____
PABA	mg	25	50	100	150	_____

Mineral	Unit	Score				Your ideal level
		0–2	3–4	5–6	7 or more	
Calcium	mg	150	300	450	600	_____
Magnesium	mg	75	150	225	300	_____
Iron	mg	10	15	20	25	_____
Zinc	mg	10	15	20	25	_____
Manganese	mg	2.5	5	10	15	_____
Selenium	mcg	25	50	75	100	_____
Chromium	mcg	20	40	80	100	_____

For example, if you initially scored three for vitamin C, but your stress check score was eight, add three points to your initial score, making it six. Using the vitamin and mineral level charts, a score of six gives you a requirement of 2,000mg of vitamin C per day. Now do the same for all the other nutrients. For vitamins B_{12}, folic acid, biotin, choline, inositol, and PABA, score half the score for the B Complex deficiency symptoms. Apart from poor memory for choline, burning in the sun for PABA, pernicious anemia for B_{12}, and increased risk of spina bifida for folic acid, research has not yet revealed specific deficiency symptoms. If any of these symptoms apply to you, add one point to the score for the relevant vitamin.

Minerals other than those in the chart are generally sufficient in most people's diets and can be increased through dietary measures. Potassium, which balances sodium (salt), is best supplied through the diet by eating plenty of raw fruit and vegetables. Phosphorus deficiency is exceedingly rare and the mineral is contained in almost all supplements as calcium phosphate. Iodine deficiency is also extremely rare. Copper is frequently oversupplied in our diets and can be toxic. A wholefood diet is almost always sufficient in copper.

How to Work Out Your Ideal Supplement Program

In case you are wondering, you don't have to take 30 different supplements every day! Your needs can be compressed into four or five different supplements, each combining the nutrients above. The most common combinations are a multivitamin (containing vitamins A, B, C, D, and E); and B Complex (which should contain vitamins B_1, B_2, B_3, B_5, B_6, B_{12}, folic acid, biotin, PABA, choline, and inositol), and a multimineral for all the minerals. Vitamin C is usually taken separately since the basic optimum requirement of 1,000mg (1g) makes quite a large tablet without adding any more nutrients. Choosing the right formula is an art in itself. Chapter 12 shows you how to read the labels and avoid the preservatives and additives that are too often used.

How Good Is Your Diet?

Many people would like to believe that as long as they take their vitamin supplements they can keep eating all the "bad" foods that they love. But you can't rely on diet, supplements, or exercise alone to keep you healthy. All three are essential.

Diet Check

Do you add sugar to food or drink almost every day?

Do you eat foods with added sugar almost every day? (read the labels carefully)

Do you use salt when cooking?

Do you add salt to your food?

Do you drink more than one cup of coffee most days?

Do you drink more than three cups of tea most days?

Do you smoke more than five cigarettes a week?

Do you take other nonmedical drugs? (e.g. cannabis, amphetamines)

Do you drink more than 1 oz of alcohol a day? (one glass of wine, 1 pint of beer, or one measure of spirits)

Do you eat fried food (e.g. bacon and eggs, french fries) more than twice a week?

Do you eat processed "fast food" more than twice
a week?
Do you eat red meat more than twice a week?
Do you often eat foods containing additives and
preservatives?
Do you eat chocolate or sweets more than twice
a week?
Does less than a third of your diet consist of raw
fruit and vegetables?
Do you drink less than ½ pint of plain water
each day?
Do you normally eat white rice or flour rather
than wholegrain?
Do you drink more than 3 pints of milk a
week?
Do you eat more than three slices of bread a day,
on average?
Are there some foods you feel "addicted" to?   _____

Score one point for each question answered yes. The maximum score is 20 and the minimum score is 0.

0 TO 4 You're obviously a health-conscious individual and
your minor indiscretions are unlikely to affect your health.
Provided you supplement your diet with the right vitamins and minerals you can look forward to a long and
healthy life.

5 TO 9 You're on the right track, but must be a little
stricter with yourself. Rather than "giving up" your bad
habits, set yourself easy experiments. For instance, for one
month go without two or three of the foods or drinks you
know are not good for you. See how you feel. Some you
may decide to have occasionally, while others you may find
you go off. But be strict for one month—your cravings are
only short-term "withdrawal" symptoms. Aim to have your
score below five within three months.

10 TO 14 Your diet is not good and you will need to make some changes to be able to reach optimum health. But take it a step at a time. You should aim to have your score down to five within six months. Start following the vitality diet, which is explained in Chapter 10. You will find that some of your bad dietary habits will change for the better as you find tasty alternatives. The "bad habits" that remain should be dealt with one at a time. Remember that sugar, salt, coffee, and chocolate are all addictive foods. Your cravings for them will dramatically decrease or go away altogether after one month without them.

15 TO 20 There is no way you can continue to eat like this and remain in good health. You are consuming far too much fat, refined foods, and artificial stimulants. Read Chapter 10 very carefully and make gradual and permanent changes to your life-style. For instance, take two questions to which you answered yes and make changes so that one month later you would answer no (one example would be to stop eating sugar and drinking coffee in the first month). Keep doing this until your score is five or less. You may feel worse for the first two weeks, but within a month you will begin to feel the positive effects of healthy eating.

10

The Vitality Diet

Before foods can give us vitality, hundreds of chemical reactions must take place involving 28 different vitamins and minerals. These micronutrients are the real keys that unlock the potential energy in our food.

Your vitality depends upon a careful balance of at least 45 nutrients. They include sources of energy or·calories that may come from carbohydrates, fats, or proteins; 13 known vitamins, 15 minerals, eight amino acids (which we get when proteins are digested), and linoleic acid, an essential nutrient in many fats. Even though the requirement for some minerals, like selenium, is less than a millionth of our requirement for protein, it is no less important. In fact, one-third of *all* chemical reactions in our bodies are dependent on tiny quantities of minerals, and even more on vitamins. Without any one of these nutrients, vitality, energy, and ideal weight are just not possible.

Fortunately, deficiency in proteins, fats, or carbohydrates is very rare. Unfortunately, deficiency in vitamins and minerals is not, despite popular belief. Many nutritionists believe that as few as one in ten people receive sufficient vitamins and minerals from their diet for optimum health.

By analyzing the typical nutrient content in a 2,500-calorie diet, we can begin to see why. The standard method of recording nutrient content is "per gram". This measurement is unhelpful, since one would eat many more grams of apple than one would of steak. All nutrient content tables record nutrients per gram and this predisposes us to select concentrated foods that are high in nutrients, such as steak, when in reality we cannot eat as much of them.

Figure 6

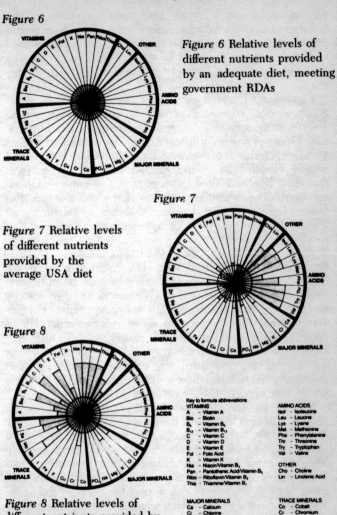

Figure 6 Relative levels of different nutrients provided by an adequate diet, meeting government RDAs

Figure 7 Relative levels of different nutrients provided by the average USA diet

Figure 7

Figure 8

Key to formula abbreviations

VITAMINS
A – Vitamin A
Bio – Biotin
B₆ – Vitamin B₆
B₁₂ – Vitamin B₁₂
C – Vitamin C
D – Vitamin D
E – Vitamin E
Fol – Folic Acid
K – Vitamin K
Nia – Niacin/Vitamin B₃
Pan – Pantothenic Acid/Vitamin B₅
Ribo – Riboflavin/Vitamin B₂
Tha – Thiamine/Vitamin B₁

AMINO ACIDS
Isol – Isoleucine
Leu – Leucine
Lys – Lysine
Met – Methionine
Phe – Phenylalanine
Thr – Threonine
Try – Tryptophan
Val – Valine

OTHER
Cho – Choline
Lin – Linolenic Acid

MAJOR MINERALS
Ca – Calcium
Cl – Chlorine
K – Potassium
Mg – Magnesium
Na – Sodium
PO₄ – Phosphate/Phosphorus

TRACE MINERALS
Co – Cobalt
Cr – Chromium
Cu – Copper
F – Fluorine
Fe – Iron
I – Iodine
Mn – Manganese
Mo – Molybdenum
Se – Selenium
Zn – Zinc

Figure 8 Relative levels of different nutrients provided by the optimum diet (there will be considerable variation from person to person)

The most important factor that stops us eating is the number of calories we have consumed.[1] All foods, whether protein or carbohydrate, or indeed fat, can be converted to supply energy. It would be wiser, therefore, to analyze the vitamin content in food "per calorie" instead of "per gram".

Figures 6, 7 and 8 each show a circle with sections. Each section represents one essential nutrient: amino acids, vitamins, major minerals, trace minerals, and others. Figure 6 shades the sections up to a line that makes an inner circle, representing a fictitious diet that would supply exactly the recommended daily levels of each nutrient. Figure 7 shows nutrients in the average American diet. Those shaded sections that do not reach the inner circle represent a nutrient shown to be deficient. Figure 8 shows the sort of optimum requirements that most people need.

As much as two-thirds of the average calorie intake is fat, sugar, and refined flours.[2] The calories in sugar are called "empty" calories because they provide no nutrients. Often hidden in processed foods and snacks, they usually weigh little and instantly satisfy our appetite. For instance, two cookies provide more calories than 1lb of carrots. They are considerably easier to eat, but they provide no vitamins or minerals. If a quarter of your diet by weight, the two-thirds by calories, consists of such dismembered foods, there's little room left to get the levels you need of the 39 essential nutrients.

Wheat, for example, has 25 nutrients removed in the refining process that turns it into white flour, yet only four (iron, B_1, B_2, B_3) are replaced. On average, 87 percent of the vital minerals zinc, chromium, and manganese are lost.[3] Have we been shortchanged? Processed meats like hamburgers and sausages are no better. The use of inferior meat high in fat lowers the nutrient content. Eggs, fish, and chicken are nutrient-rich sources of protein, but protein deficiency is rarely a problem.

Vegetables, fruits, nuts, and seeds are full of vitality. Tomatoes and lettuce, for example, are packed with vitamins and minerals. The humble potato is also vitality rich, but make sure you eat potatoes with their skins on. Other excellent foods are peas (best source of manganese for vegetarians); bananas (high in potassium); mushrooms; spinach and other green leafy vegetables; beans; nuts and lentils. Foods such as these should make up at least half of your diet.

Eating for Vitality

One secret of longer life, greater energy, *and* less weight is to eat foods high in vitamin and mineral vitality. But this is not the only criterion for judging a food to be good. Good food should also be low in fat, salt, and fast-releasing sugars; high in fiber, and alkaline-forming. Nonanimal sources of protein are desirable. Such a diet will also be low in calories, but then you won't have to count them, because your body will become increasingly efficient and will not crave extra food. Craving for food when you have eaten enough calories is often a craving for more nutrients, so foods providing "empty" calories are strictly to be avoided. The list below tells you which foods are good and bad from all these different points of view.

ALKALINE-FORMING FOODS all fresh fruit and vegetables; millet; almonds; brazil nuts; herb teas; yogurt; bean sprouts.

SLOW-RELEASING SUGARS fresh and dried fruit; wholemeal

LOW FAT FOODS white fish; seafood; low fat yogurt and cheese; skimmed milk; soy milk; tofu; beans; vegetables; fruit.

ACID-FORMING FOODS beans; all meat and fish; grains; most nuts; seeds; milk produce; tea; coffee; chocolate; sugar; fats.

NON-MEAT PROTEIN FOODS milk; cheese; yogurt; eggs; beans; rice; lentils; nuts; seeds; tofu.

HIGH FAT FOODS meat; dairy produce, including butter, cheese and ice cream; margarine; vegetable oils.

MEAT PROTEIN all meat, e.g. beef, pork, lamb; also chicken and fish.

UNREFINED FOODS nuts; seeds; wholegrains; wholemeal flour and bread; lentils; beans; brown rice. molasses; maple syrup; glucose and most syrups.

FAST-RELEASING SUGARS white, brown, and raw sugar; grains, e.g. muesli and brown rice; honey.

HIGH SODIUM FOODS salt, including sea salt; yeast extracts; all smoked fish; some cheeses; potato chips; salted nuts; most canned foods; soy sauce.

HIGH POTASSIUM FOODS fruit, including pineapples, grapes, and bananas; vegetables; dandelion coffee; chicory coffee.

REFINED FOODS white flour; white, brown, and raw sugar; white rice; processed and most packaged foods.

The following ideas and recipes by Liz Holford will help you to change to a more healthy and enjoyable diet. As you become familiar with new foods (there are, for example, over twelve different kinds of beans), variety will never be a problem. Some suggestions are for "instant" snacks when time is short; others are for proper meals. All are tried and tested and easy to make.

Sunshine Breakfasts

Starting the day with a meal based on protein and complex carbohydrates will give you a stable blood sugar and energy level throughout the day. Yogurt makes an ideal early-morning protein as it is already partly digested. But fruit yogurts from supermarkets have a high sugar content, not to mention numerous stabilizers, colorings, flavorings, and preservatives, so choose good, natural, "live" yogurt. "Live" yogurt has not been pasteurized to increase shelf-life—a process that reduces the bacteria in it that promote a healthy small intestine.

Liven up your natural yogurt with some of the following: bananas; sunflower seeds; ground sesame seeds; wheat germ; chopped apple, pear, or any other fruit in season; desiccated coconut; almonds (whole, chopped, or ground); cashews; hazel nuts; raisins, apricots, or any other dried fruit that you enjoy.

Eggs are another way to get your morning protein; boiled or poached eggs are best since they don't·involve fat. Enjoy them with wholemeal toast, rice cakes (available from health food shops), oatcakes, or whole rye crisp-breads.

Muesli, being an uncooked complex carbohydrate, is a good start to the day. It can be made even more nourishing by adding plenty of nuts and seeds (sunflower and ground sesame seeds). Alternatively, you can make your own "muesli" solely out of your favorite nuts, seeds, and dried and fresh fruit. Muesli can be eaten with any combination of skimmed milk, yogurt, soy milk, or fruit juice—apple juice is particularly tasty. Always remember that muesli can be sweetened quite adequately with dried or fresh fruit or fruit juice, so *never* buy a commercial muesli that has added sugar.

Alternatives to Tea and Coffee

Herb teas are both refreshing and relaxing. The number of different flavors available in convenient tea bags is so large that you could have a different drink every day for a month! I highly recommend that you experiment with the different varieties and find one that suits your taste. Some of the most delicious ones are mixtures with names such as Lemon Mist, Red Zinger, Emperor's Choice, and Almond Sunset. Peppermint, rosehip, mixed fruit, and lemon verbena come a close second, while rooibosch ("red bush"—a common tea in Africa) is often a good starting point as it is most like Indian tea in flavor and can be taken with milk.

If you are a coffee drinker then some of the coffee substitutes may suit you better. Again the choice is large and you should not give up until you've tried them all! Dandelion coffee and chicory are both very high in potassium, chicory having the "bitter" taste of coffee. Barleycup is very popular and is a good one to try first. Decaffeinated coffee is one stage better than ordinary coffee, but no decaffeinated coffee has *all* the caffeine removed and it still contains other stimulants present in coffee. Remember also that numerous chemicals are used in the decaffeinating process.

The following two drinks are more substantial than herb tea or coffee and can even make a delicious, light breakfast.

Summer Fruit Cocktail

YOU WILL NEED
8oz (225g) fresh fruit. Some delicious combinations that work well are:
   a banana and a grated apple
   an orange and a banana
   strawberries, raspberries, blueberries
   a nectarine or a peach and an orange
2 tbs desiccated coconut
½ tsp natural vanilla essence
ice

HOW TO MAKE IT
Chop the fruit into small pieces and put it in a blender or food processor. Add the coconut, vanilla essence, and ice. Liquidize into a puree, adding a little water if necessary. Add enough water to make the puree into a pouring consistency. Enjoy your summer fruit cocktail with whole pieces of fruit on a cocktail stick in a tall glass.

Real Fruit Thick Milk Shake

YOU WILL NEED
4oz (125g) fresh fruit, using the combinations given for summer fruit cocktail (above)
1½ pints (300 ml) skimmed milk or sugar-free soy milk
2 tbs ground almonds
2 tbs desiccated coconut
ice

HOW TO MAKE IT
Chop the fruit into small pieces and put it in a blender or food processor with the almonds, coconut, and ice. Liq-

uidize into a puree, then add milk and liquidize further. Taste and add honey or maple syrup if desired. Enjoy it in a tall glass with a straw.

Practical Lunches

At Home
The fastest "convenience" food has to be a salad—you don't even need to turn an oven on, and it's a meal that scores ten out of ten for vitality. Make a simpler version than the one given for a dinner (p. 110), choosing as many different vegetables as time allows. If you mix one of the salad dressings in a larger quantity than you need, it can be kept in the refrigerator and used as necessary. You can also use any of the ideas in the "At Work" section.

At Work
The following salads are ones that can be made the night before and kept in the refrigerator, or made in the morning, and taken to work in a plastic container. The mayonnaise can be made in large quantities and will keep very well for up to a week in the refrigerator.

Coleslaw

YOU WILL NEED
8oz (225g) white or red cabbage
4oz (125g) carrots
2oz (50g) onion
2oz (50g) walnuts
2oz (50g) raisins
mayonnaise dressing (p. 111)

HOW TO MAKE IT
Finely chop or shred all the raw vegetables. Add the nuts, raisins, and enough mayonnaise to cover. These quantities are enough for two people.

Potato Salad

YOU WILL NEED
1lb (450g) cold boiled potatoes
4 blades fresh chives (use dried if fresh not available)
mayonnaise dressing (p. 111)

HOW TO MAKE IT
Dice the potatoes, chop the chives, and add enough
mayonnaise to coat the potatoes. This can be made into a
more substantial meal by adding a chopped hard-boiled
egg or 1oz (25g) of cheddar cheese.

Salad Dips

YOU WILL NEED
A selection of the following vegetables: carrots, celery,
cucumber, red or green peppers, French beans, radishes,
cauliflower florets and spring onions.
mayonnaise dressing, without milk (p. 111), or avocado dip.

Avocado dip:
1 ripe avocado
2 tbs natural yogurt
dried mixed herbs
freshly ground pepper

HOW TO MAKE IT
Mash the avocado with a fork and mix in the other dip
ingredients. Serve with sticks of the fresh, raw vegetables.

Baked Potatoes

Fill a baked potato with one of the following nourishing
fillings that you can take to work in a plastic container:

shrimp and chopped tomatoes
grated cheese, chopped apple, and celery
cottage cheese and cucumber
tuna fish, chopped cucumber, tomato, and pepper

Fresh fruit or dried fruit and nuts make a good finish to any of these meals.

Nourishing Nibbles

Without doubt fresh fruit is the most nourishing of nibbles, followed closely by mixtures of dried fruit and nuts. Almond-stuffed figs: push an almond firmly into the center of each fig. Walnuts and dates are a good combination. A wedge of cheese with dates or an apple make for a more substantial snack.

Tea-Time Tempters

Honey and Walnut Delights

YOU WILL NEED
for pastry:
6oz (175g) wholemeal flour
4oz (125g) softened butter
ice-cold water

for filling:
honey
chopped walnuts

HOW TO MAKE THEM
Cut the butter into the flour with a knife until a crumblike consistency is achieved. Bind with the water, then roll out and cut into circles to line tartlet tins. Fill each circle of pastry with a teaspoon of chopped walnuts and a teaspoon of honey. Bake for about 25 minutes, or until brown, at 350°F (175°C).

Eat the honey and walnut delights on their own or topped with natural yogurt.

Marzipan Dates

YOU WILL NEED
dates
4oz (125g) ground almonds
1 small egg, lightly beaten
1 tbs honey
whole almonds

HOW TO MAKE THEM
Combine the ground almonds, beaten egg, and honey to make a paste. Split the dates and fill them with the almond paste. Top each stuffed date with a whole almond.

Dinners

For maximum vitality you should ensure that the main meal of your day consists of a large, fresh, raw salad. Nearly every vegetable available can be eaten raw—experiment! Delicious ones to use are: carrots, cucumber, crisp lettuce, beets, peppers, mustard and cress, watercress, French beans, avocados, carrot tops, fennel, red and white cabbage, zucchini, tomatoes, celery, and—last but not least—bean sprouts. Bean sprouts make the freshest of salads are are easily grown on any window sill either in a salad sprouter (available from your local health food shop) or in a jam jar with a piece of muslin tied over the top. Simply cover the seeds (alfalfa and mung are the easiest to sprout, although any whole pulse or seed can be used) with water twice a day then drain off excess water. The seeds should sprout within four to seven days.

A salad is made into a meal with a good dressing and accompanying protein dishes.

French Dressing

YOU WILL NEED
6 tbs vegetable oil (olive, sunflower, or safflower)

3 tbs cider vinegar
1 clove of garlic, crushed or very finely chopped
1 tsp mustard powder
2 tsp mixed herbs, fresh if available
freshly ground black pepper

HOW TO MAKE IT
Put all the ingredients in a screw-top jar and shake them together vigorously.

Mayonnaise Dressing

YOU WILL NEED
2 tbs ready-prepared mayonnaise
2 tbs natural yogurt
1 tbs skimmed milk
dried mixed herbs
freshly ground black pepper

HOW TO MAKE IT
Mix the ingredients thoroughly with a fork, or put them in a screw-top jar and shake vigorously.

"Any Vegetable" Soup

YOU WILL NEED
1½lb (675g) chopped fresh vegetables, e.g. carrots, celery, leeks, zucchini, tomatoes, cauliflower
1 medium onion
1 low-salt vegetable stock cube (available from health food shops)
2 tsp mixed herbs

HOW TO MAKE IT
Slice the onion and simmer it in a little water until it is soft. Add the chopped vegetables (a combination of the

above or one single one can be used), herbs, and the stock cube. Cover with water and simmer until all the vegetables are just soft. Liquidize or puree and serve the soup hot.

Millet Burgers

YOU WILL NEED
1 large onion
3oz (75g) cheddar cheese
6oz (150g) cooked millet grain or flakes
¼ tsp mustard powder
1 egg, lightly beaten
freshly ground pepper
1 tsp thyme
1 tsp marjoram
butter

HOW TO MAKE THEM
Finely chop the onion and grate the cheese, and combine them with the cooked millet, herbs, ground pepper, mustard powder, and beaten egg. Form into patties, dot with a little butter and put under a medium to hot grill for 10 minutes. Turn them, putting a little butter on the other side, and cook for a further 10 minutes. Serve the millet burgers with a tomato salad and coleslaw (p. 107).

Chick-Pea, Egg, and Tuna Feast

YOU WILL NEED
6oz (150g) chick peas, soaked overnight and boiled until tender (about 45 minutes)
3 hard-boiled eggs, roughly chopped
1 small onion, finely chopped
7oz (200g) tuna fish, flaked
1 tbs vinegar
2 tbs cold-pressed vegetable oil

freshly ground black pepper
3 tbs chopped parsley
1 tbs chopped chives
½ tsp mustard powder

HOW TO MAKE IT
Mix the cooked chick-peas, hard-boiled eggs, tuna, and onion together. Put the vinegar, oil, pepper, mustard, chives, and parsley in a screw-top jar and shake vigorously. Pour this dressing over the chick-pea mixture and decorate with sprigs of fresh parsley. Serve with potato salad or baked potatoes, tomato or mixed salad.

Fish Pie

YOU WILL NEED
10oz (250g) any white fish
8oz (225g) shrimp
10oz (250g) smoked haddock, free from artificial coloring
4oz (125g) mushrooms, sliced
1oz (25g) butter
1 tbs wholemeal flour
½ pint (300ml) skimmed milk
2 tsp mixed herbs
freshly ground pepper
2lb (900g) potatoes, boiled and mashed with pepper and a
    little skimmed milk
4oz (125g) grated cheese

HOW TO MAKE IT
Steam the white fish and the haddock for 15 minutes. Meanwhile make a white sauce in the usual way using the butter, wholemeal flour, and milk. Gently mix together the steamed fish, shrimp, sauce, sliced mushrooms, mixed herbs, and pepper. Put in an ovenproof dish. Spread the

mashed potatoes on top of the fish mixture. Sprinkle the grated cheese on top and bake the pie for 30 minutes at 400°F (200°C). Serve with mixed salad and peas.

Stuffed Eggplant

YOU WILL NEED
1 medium-sized eggplant
1 cup of brown rice
4oz (125g) mushrooms, chopped
8oz (225g) tomatoes, chopped
1 medium onion, chopped
1 low-salt vegetable stock cube
2 tsp mixed herbs
6oz (150g) chopped hazelnuts or almonds
6oz (150g) grated cheese

HOW TO MAKE IT
Bring 2½ cups of water to the boil, add the rice and boil for 45 minutes. Meanwhile simmer the chopped onion in a little water in a frying pan until it is just soft, add the mushrooms and tomatoes, the stock cube and mixed herbs. Cook for a further two minutes. Cut the eggplant in half lengthwise; scoop out the seeds and soft pulp. Combine the cooked rice, vegetable mixture and the nuts, and pile the mixture in the center of the eggplant halves. Place the eggplant halves in a roasting bag and bake for 30 minutes, or until soft, at 400°F (200°C). Remove the eggplant halves from the roasting bag, sprinkle cheese on top and brown them under the broiler. Serve with a mixed salad.

The same stuffing can be used to stuff peppers, tomatoes, or zucchini.

Other suggestions for healthy dinners are vegetarian lasagna, soufflés, quiches, and nut roasts. You will find recipes for these in most good wholefood cookbooks.

Desserts to Surprise You

You will be surprised at how often fresh or dried fruit can be used to sweeten desserts instead of sugar. Have a look at your favorite recipes for cakes, puddings, and desserts and ask yourself if you could substitute wholemeal flour for white; substitute raisins, dried apricots, dates, or fresh bananas for any sugar, golden syrup, glucose, brown sugar, or honey; substitute honey or maple syrup for sugar and, at the same time, reduce the amount used. Here are some suggestions for healthy desserts.

Fruit Fool

YOU WILL NEED
8oz (225g) low-fat cottage cheese
8fl.oz (225g) natural yogurt
1lb (450g) boysenberries, stewed with 4oz (125g)
    or 8oz (225g) stewed dried apricots
    or 1lb (450g) strawberries
    or 8oz (225g) stewed blueberries and 1 chopped banana
¼ tsp natural vanilla essence
2 egg whites

HOW TO MAKE IT
Prepare the fruit as indicated. Put all the ingredients except the egg whites in a blender or food processor and liquidize. Whisk the egg whites and fold them into the mixture. Put the fool in an attractive bowl or individual glasses and leave it in the refrigerator until it is needed. Arrange whole pieces of fruit on top of the fool before serving.

Rice Pudding

YOU WILL NEED
1½oz (45g) short-grain brown rice
1 pint (600ml) skimmed milk
2oz (50g) sultanas
ground nutmeg

HOW TO MAKE IT
Put the rice and sultanas into a greased overproof dish, pour on the milk and sprinkle with nutmeg. Bake for two hours, or until the rice is soft, at 300°F (150°C).

Fruit Salad

Cut into cubes any fruit that is in season. Pour over it an apricot sauce, made by stewing 2oz (50g) dried apricots and liquidizing them with enough extra water to make into a pourable sauce.

Serve with yogurt cream, made by mixing equal quantities of whipped cream and natural yogurt, or cashew cream, made by pureeing ground cashews with enough water to make a pourable sauce.

11

Exercise for Life

Every morning, Gladys and Dorothy Sharp set out to visit their sister and take her dog for a walk. Nothing remarkable in that? Well, they walk the entire route: a total of 13 miles a day, 65 miles a week. And these live-wire twins are 73 years old!

To many, this *does* seems a remarkable feat. It is not: Gladys and Dorothy are doing only what we are all capable of doing. Blissfully ignorant about training programs and exercise classes, they are still following the most important principles of exercise, and reaping the most important rewards. Clearly, they are both extremely fit and healthy. But there are more subtle benefits too. Both are happy, and content with life. They look forward to each day, and find pleasure even in simple experiences like smiling at the people they meet and enjoying the countryside they walk through. Their actions say more about exercise than words ever could. Above all, they provide a living demonstration of the two most important principles of exercise:

1. Exercise is for *all* of us.
2. Exercise is for life.

The 1980s have seen an explosion of interest in exercise—it has become one of the fashions of the decade. Glossy magazines promote fitness and vitality and associate exercise with beauty and glamour. But, as with most fashions, this type of thinking tends to exclude more people than it includes. It's time to step back from the fashion image. What are the *real* reasons why exercise is so important? What are the *real* benefits?

Promoting Good Health

A certain level of activity is essential to health. Most of us fail to reach that level. Advances in technology mean that more and more people have sedentary jobs and use their leisure in passive ways, like watching television. These are relatively recent changes, and have overtaken our evolutionary ability to adapt to them. Not so long ago, day-to-day living provided plenty of walking, stretching, lifting, and carrying. The human body is designed to be active, and it hasn't changed!

Today's inactive life-style slowly damages a whole range of body systems. Joints become stiff and degenerate with age if they are under-used. Muscles lose their strength and flexibility and can look flabby without regular exercise. Even bones can lose calcium and become weak and brittle—a condition known as osteoporosis—because inactive people excrete more calcium in their urine than active people: this, coupled with a poor diet, can mean that not enough calcium is available to maintain proper levels in the skeleton.[1]

The cardiovascular system, in particular the heart, needs regular exercise to stay in optimum condition. It has not yet been conclusively proved that exercise prevents the clogged arteries, which lead to heart failure,[2] but it does do three things that increase the reserve capacity of the whole system. It improves the efficiency with which the blood carries oxygen to provide energy; it improves the body's ability to use that oxygen, and it increases the blood supply to the heart itself so that it can cope much better when extra stress is placed on it. That's why regular exercise will decrease your chance of suffering a heart attack by about 50 percent.[3]

Coping with Stress

Today's life-style may lack activity, but it does not lack stress. Here again, we have evolved too fast to develop new ways to cope. The caveman, faced with a fierce-looking wild animal, experienced a number of physiological changes. Glucose was released into his bloodstream and his breathing become more rapid to provide more oxygen. His heartbeat also rose, to transfer these energy-making nutrients to his muscles at a faster rate. His skin pores dilated and he started to sweat, to maximize his cooling capacity. These body reactions set him up for the most appropriate action—100 meters in 10.8 seconds!

The business executive, late for an important appointment and held up by yet another traffic jam, experiences the same changes as the caveman. But he does not have the appropriate means to respond: a long, loud blast on the horn is the nearest he can get to being physically active. Stressful situations of this kind, repeated many times without release of an appropriate response, can lead to overload of the systems. The body then "adapts" to stress in order to cope with these inappropriate physiological changes. But it does this at a price. Associated with high-stress living are a host of minor ills, including headaches, stiffness, infections, insomnia, digestive complaints, and moodiness. This is the state that many sedentary westerners experience throughout their whole lives. For some, the unnatural adaptation can be maintained; for others, it eventually becomes too much and leads to more serious complaints, including heart disease, diabetes, arthritis, and even cancer.

Can exercise help to prevent this vicious cycle? Although in many cases exercise is not possible at the appropriate moment, the answer is yes. A life style that includes steady, rhythmic exercise, coupled with relaxation and stress-reducing techniques, is less likely to bring on the cumulative effects associated with repeated stress.

Controlling Your Weight

As a nation, we are actually decreasing our intake of food, yet the maintenance of a healthy weight is becoming increasingly difficult for more and more people. Lack of exercise is a major contribution to this problem. In the active life-style for which our species was designed, people needed over 4,000 calories a day just to provide enough energy for living. Appetite and other physiological systems were geared to achieving this kind of intake.

Most people now lead lives which require far less food than this, but their appetite mechanisms have not adjusted. Many people fail to maintain their optimum weight, or manage to do so only by suppressing their natural appetite. The natural solution to this problem is exercise. Research has shown that the appetite of very active people is often for fewer calories than they expend, while the appetite of inactive people is for more.[4] The message is clear—if you enjoy food and have a tendency to put on weight, exercise is the only solution!

Exercise provides an additional bonus. Many books give tables showing how a given amount of exercise will burn up a given quantity of calories. But that is not the whole story. If exercise is vigorous enough, it will raise your metabolism—the rate at which you burn calories—for up to 15 hours.[5] So by taking regular daily exercise you can permanently raise your metabolic rate and therefore lose weight faster.

Enjoying Exercise

For many people, the long-term benefits are not enough to encourage them to start exercising. The very thought of it is a turn-off. It's boring, painful, difficult, time-consuming, or even embarrassing. If this is how you think, you have probably never exercised, or you have been taught very badly.

Instead, try thinking about having a body that feels good, looks attractive, and gives you a heightened self-image. Think about feeling happier and enjoying life to the full. Think about having more vitality and zest for living. Exercise is a readily accessible way of achieving these things. Runners don't make better lovers just because they have more stamina, but because they have a heightened awareness of the good things in life!

A number of researchers have found a link between regular exercise and increased feelings of well-being and happiness. Dr. Thaddeus Kostrubala, author of *The Joy of*

Running, has used aerobic exercise successfully in the treatment of depression,[6] and Dr. Kenneth Cooper, the inventor of the word "aerobic", found in his exercise programs for the US Air Force that the vast majority of his subjects felt more positive and enthusiastic about life.[7] Exactly why this happens is still unclear, but it seems that during exercise the body releases more endorphins— morphinelike substances that give you a natural "high".

Fitness Versus Health

If the thought of taking exercise still puts you off, you have probably come to associate it purely with improving fitness. You look at the exhausting training schedules followed by top athletes and think, "If that's what exercise is all about, then it's not for me!"

But optimum fitness is not the same thing as optimum health. Fitness is concerned with developing *maximum* physical capacity, a delicate balance-point which can easily be overstepped, leading to staleness and loss of vitality. Many top athletes have made this mistake. At some stage in their careers, they put too much into their training at a time when their other body systems are below par. Their performance then deteriorates, and often they counter this by yet more training, pushing the body well beyond its limits. The results are injury or illness, disillusionment and depression.

But good health is not about achieving *maximum* physical capacity; it is about developing the body's systems to cope with all the demands of life, and to enjoy them. By changing your priority from fitness to health, you open up a whole new perspective. Exercise changes from being a boring routine of painful or exhausting training sessions to a varied program of activity aimed at maximizing enjoyment and achieving high-level health in the broadest sense.

The benefits of exercise are affected by the amount, or the intensity, of your exercise sessions. For some types of activity, a threshold level must be reached before the exercise has any significant benefit.[8] Most sedentary people fail to pass this threshold. Once it is passed, however, the benefits increase rapidly for only a small amount of extra effort. After that things start to level out, because you have reached the optimum stage. Maximum benefit and fitness can then be achieved only by raising your exercise level considerably. If you continue to increase the amount or the intensity beyond this optimum range, you may even do yourself harm.

The BLISSS exercise program in this chapter is designed to help you reach the optimum stage—a level that does much to prevent the ill health suffered by sedentary people. The BLISSS target range is the most efficient level for people whose time for exercise is limited but who want to feel healthy, alive, and active, and to do as much as possible to prevent ill health.

Making a Start—The *P* Principles

For most people, getting started is the biggest hurdle to regular exercise. Many runners find it harder to decide to go running, get their shoes on, and go out the front door than they do to run! What you want is a program that will last you for life, so it's especially important to get rid of some of the psychological barriers that can trip up the unsuspecting. The biggest of these is ignorance of the way that mind and body adjust to exercise. Three basic principles underlie any successful exercise program: understand and follow them, and you'll avoid many of the common mistakes that could stand between you and your program for life.

Patience

Many people lost interest in exercise because their bodies do not adapt quickly enough, or they are not aware that changes are taking place. You will *not* notice changes on a day-to-day basis. Genuine adaptation to exercise is a comparatively slow process. But the improvement will be there if you stand back and compare your vitality and fitness levels over a period of at least a month or two.

No single training session can make any significant

difference to your health. The training process needs patience because the benefits build up gradually. Change your perspective a little. Stop seeing exercise in small isolated parts, and start seeing improvements to health as an overall life process.

Progress

Few people apply the progress principle to best effect. Many start with an excess of enthusiasm, and try to achieve a level that places too much stress on the body. This usually leads to pain or exhaustion, destroying enthusiasm and leading to a high dropout rate. Those who do persevere, on the other hand, may find that they stick at a constant level and feel they are stagnating.

One of the best things in a good program is the sense of achievement you can get from gradual, but continuous, improvement. The ideal program for life, then, starts at a level that is within your capabilities and then raises those capabilities steadily without ever exceeding them. There is no pain and no exhaustion, but you see yourself getting fitter and healthier.

Perseverance

To continue to enjoy the health benefits of an exercise program, you must keep on doing it. To persevere with something one doesn't really enjoy may be possible for some people, but it is not the true way to aim at optimum health. Don't look at exercise as an obligation that *must* be done. Take some thought and design a program that suits your own tastes. Exercise should be an enjoyable habit that fits neatly into your personal daily routine. This does not mean, however, that every single training session will be enjoyable! The first sessions will probably be uncomfortable as your sedentary body adjusts to something new. After you have adapted, some sessions will still be less enjoyable than others, for a whole variety of reasons. But when enjoyment disappears from most, or all, of the sessions, then it's time to redesign your program.

Exercise Is Blisss!

The key to a successful exercise program, then, is to base it on your own needs and preferences. The BLISSS program aims to do just that—to give you the information you need to choose your own activities, and enable you to know that they are giving you the maximum benefit in the minimum time.

The explanation for what the BL in BLISSS stands for comes a bit later. The I stands for "individualize", and it belongs in the very center of your program. But before you can choose your program, you need to know what you are aiming at—the SSS factors at the end of it all.

The Three *S* Factors

Exercise is very specific in the effects it has on the body. The benefits gained reflect precisely the characteristics of the exercise carried out. Say you exercise your left arm by lifting a heavy weight a few times, and exercise your right arm by lifting a light weight a great many times. Your left are will develop strength, but not stamina; your right arm will develop stamina, but not strength. Your legs won't develop at all! This may seem obvious, but it is a much neglected point. To develop all-round health and well-being you need to work on all three of the main types of exercise: stamina, suppleness, and strength.

Stamina

Stamina, or endurance, is the ability to exercise at a moderate level for a long time without becoming exhausted or out of breath. Stamina exercises improve the endurance of the heart, lungs, and circulation, and their ability to recover from exertion. These are the most important factors in reducing the risk of cardiovascular disease, including heart failure and stroke. So, for better health, specific stamina training is essential.

To improve stamina, you need regular, aerobic exercise lasting at least 20 to 30 minutes at a time.[9] For exercise to be aerobic (which literally means "with oxygen"), enough oxygen must be provided for the activity *while you are doing it*. If you get out of breath so much that you have to stop the activity or reduce its intensity, you are building up an "oxygen debt" and you are exercising "anaerobically", without sufficient oxygen. Anaerobic exercise, such as a top-speed sprint that leaves you gasping, puts an excessive strain on the body and cannot be continued for long. So it cannot provide the steady but continuous 20 to 30 minutes' exercise that will train your heart to develop optimum stamina.

To make too little effort, however, is as useless as to make too much. The easiest way to check your level is to take your pulse and make sure your heart is working neither too fast nor too slowly. Most people should aim to achieve a pulse rate of between 110 and 160 beats per minute, depending on age and fitness. This represents a level of intensity when you are breathing harder, but you are still able to talk!

Once your pulse is raised to your target level, keep it there without any rests or breaks for 20 to 30 minutes. For the beginner, it is often best to build up gradually to this extended period, starting with a short period of gentle exercise and then increasing both the intensity and the duration. A fit person should be able to maintain aerobic exercise for two hours or more. To choose the exercise that is best and most enjoyable for you, see p. 131.

To determine your target heart rate for optimum training while exercising, follow these steps:

1. Find your resting heart rate by counting your pulse for one minute.
2. Determine your maximum heart rate (MHR) by subtracting your age from 220 if you are a man or 226 if you are a woman.
3. Figure your target rate zone by taking both 65 percent and 80 percent of your MHR.

Or use this formula: Maximum Heart Rate (MHR) − Resting Heart Rate × Desired Percentage of Maximum Heart Rate + Current Resting Heart Rate = Training Heart Rate.

Suppleness

Suppleness, or flexibility, is a measure of the maximum range of movement you can achieve in your joints and muscles. It declines with age more readily than the other two S factors, and it is vital in keeping you young as long as possible. Inactive people can look, and feel, much older than they are once they start losing the ability to bend, stretch, and turn with ease.

Supple, well-stretched muscles can also reduce stiffness at any age, and prevent aches and pains. If you are taking vigorous exercise, stretching reduces the chances of injury and should always form part of your warm-up routine. But don't copy certain well-known fitness stars who stretch by jerking. Fast repetitions of toe-touching and similar exercises do not promote the maximum range of movement, and they carry a risk of injury. Muscles have a built-in safety mechanism called the stretch reflex, which makes the muscle contract if it has been stretched too quickly to its maximum.[10] Jerky, bouncing stretches override this mechanism by sheer momentum or body weight, and this can lead to long-term muscle damage.

The safe, effective way to stretch is to do it slowly to your limit of flexibility, and then to hold the stretch for five to ten seconds. The muscle then adjusts to this limit and relaxes, allowing you to take the stretch a little further. Slow stretching therefore allows you to extend your range of movement and become more and more flexible.

Yoga is an excellent way to improve suppleness, and stretch sessions are incorporated into many keep-fit and dance classes. Since they need little space, take little time, and make no noise, suppleness exercises are ideal to do at home. See p. 134 for a suppleness program you can do by yourself, or use it to check that your chosen stretch class is covering all the main body areas where you need to keep supple.

Strength

Strength training for health is quite different from strength training for maximum fitness. An athlete who aims for maximum strength will spend hours lifting weights and acquire a very muscular body. Most people do not have the time or the inclination for this level of strength and it is certainly not needed for optimum health. In our machine-based society, superstrength is rather a redundant asset.

But a certain degree of muscle tone is vital for good looks. Even if you have no excess body fat at all, underused muscles will droop and bulge and make you look flabby. Stronger muscles will firm you up, as well as making it easier and more pleasant to carry out your daily activities.

Strength exercises are also important to basic good health. The body is a rigid skeleton supported by the muscles, which are held in tension to stop the whole structure collapsing. If some of these muscles are too weak, or if pairs of muscles that work together get out of balance, the whole body can get out of balance and various conditions such as hiatus hernia can develop.

Many sports and hobbies have the potential to develop strength. So do everyday chores that involve lifting, pulling, and pushing. See p. 138 for a basic strength program you can do quickly and easily at home, or use it as a checklist to make sure that, as a matter of routine, you make some effort with *all* of the muscles covered by the exercises.

Blisss—The Beginning

Now you know what exercise is all about, you can start putting that knowledge together to make your own personal program for life. Remember—no exercise program will give you optimum health unless it covers *all* the major aspects—the three S factors. The BLISSS program makes sure nothing is left out.

The easiest, most convenient starting point for any program is your basic, day-to-day life-style. For many people, that's where the trouble first begins, as technology ensures that more and more activities need no more effort than sitting down and pressing a switch. While this has many advantages, freeing us to do more interesting and worthwhile things, it is very easy to let the "convenience" option take over completely. Think about it. How often do you take the soft option when the more active alternative is just as quick and enjoyable?

So the beginning of BLISSS is BL for base-line. The effort involved is very small—you simply start with a change of attitude. Raise your base level of activity in a hundred little ways by choosing the "active" option in small, everyday things. Each small, active choice will contribute little exercise benefit on its own but, added up over a lifetime, they will make an enormous difference to your physical health and your self-image. You will become a person who is lively and capable, rather than passive and helpless. Look at the list of examples—and start adding your own.

Passive way	Active way
Take the elevator	Use the stairs
Use a shopping cart	Use hand baskets
Drive to work	Cycle or walk at least part of the way
Buy/cook convenience food	Buy/cook fresh food
Watch television	Take up an active hobby
Use remote control for television/video recorder	Get up and press the button
Use powered tools for cooking, gardening, work	Do it by hand when it's quicker
Amuse children by turning on television	Amuse children by playing with them

Blisss—The Middle

You have already started to choose your own, individual options with your base-line *(BL)* list. That's what puts the "I" in BLISSS. Now apply the same principle a little further.

Individualize some more. Base-line activities make a firm foundation for your program. But unless your job or life-style make unusual physical demands, it will not bring you to your optimum exercise target level.

Most people will benefit greatly by adding specific exercise sessions to each day. These sessions should concentrate the benefits of a fully active day into a much shorter period of time, and thus be balanced between working on the three S factors and getting the maximum results in the minimum time.

But these sessions must provide one more thing— enjoyment. This is where you come into the picture as an individual. Don't adopt a routine program. Think carefully about what gives *you* pleasure—never mind what other people enjoy or suggest. Obviously you will have to do your own thinking at this point, but here are some factors you might like to consider.

Competition

Are you a competitive type? If so, a competitive setting can give you a great sense of pride and boost your self-esteem as you train to achieve optimum performance. Don't forget that you can compete against your own past achievements as well as against other people. But beware of the pitfalls. It is impossible to go on improving all the time, and it is impossible to win all the time. If competition is your sole focus, the end is certain to be disillusionment and an early retirement!

Variety

If you are dedicated to a single sport or type of exercise, check that it is not developing one S factor, or one part of the body, at the expense of others. For most people, variety is the spice of life. By choosing a different type of exercise each day, it is much easier to avoid boredom and to get whole body development on both physical and mental levels. Again, beware of the pitfalls. For the beginner, it will obviously take longer to adapt fully to each type of exercise. And it may not be possible for you to attain maximum performance in any of them.

Sociability
If you are a gregarious type, exercising with other people is a good chance for a pleasant get-together. Exercising with other people also increases your motivation to keep going with a certain schedule. But beware of too much inter-group competition—while it may provide an ego-boost for some, for others it can reinforce a sense of failure.

Mental Relaxation
Exercise provides an opportunity to switch off from all your problems, especially if you have a high-pressure job. Associating exercise with relaxation in this way reinforces your enjoyment.

Awareness
One of the most rewarding things about regular exercise is the heightened awareness and ease of movement you achieve, especially after 30 to 40 minutes of aerobic exercise. If you happen to be in beautiful surroundings when it happens, it's an experience to be savored for a long time afterward. But don't expect it to happen at once. You need to reach a certain level of fitness to make it possible.

Confidence
It is essential to believe, at a deep level, that regular exercise is a vital part of optimum health. Do all you can to reinforce that confidence. There will always be times when the other attractions of exercise temporarily disappear, and this confidence will be all that remains. It must be rock solid!

Blisss—The End

Armed with a real understanding of why you want to exercise, you can now custom-build your own specialist exercise sessions to cover the three vital *S* factors. The BLISSS maintenance schedule is the minimum you will need to reach your target for stamina, suppleness, and strength. It is not meant to be followed as a rigorous routine, but to give a basic feel for the principles of exercise. As you make progress, you will want to vary the sessions with exercises of your own.

Just one thing should never vary: every session should start with a five-minute warm-up, to loosen muscles and joints and reduce the risk of straining or tearing. Five minutes of suppleness exercises should be followed by a gentle progression to raise the heart rate to aerobic training level.

Blisss Maintenance Schedule

Day 1 Warm-up (five minutes) + stamina session (25 minutes)

Day 2 Suppleness and strength session (20 minutes)

Day 3 Warm-up (five minutes) + stamina session (25 minutes)

Day 4 Suppleness and strength session (20 minutes)

Day 5 Warm-up (five minutes) + stamina session (25 minutes)

Day 6 Suppleness and strength session (20 minutes)

Day 7 Activity session—from one hour to all day!

Stamina

When choosing your stamina (aerobic) exercise, remember the basic requirements:

1. You must be able to maintain it without a pause for a long time (20 to 30 minutes). Start with shorter sessions of five to ten minutes, then increase duration. Last, increase the pace.
2. It must be intense enough to raise your pulse to 110 to 160 beats per minute.
3. It should carry a low risk of injury. A warm-up will help.

Swimming

Swimming satisfies all these criteria. The water supports your weight, and so eliminates any risk of injury (apart from drowning!) But swimming really means swimming—

not paddling or sitting on the side. For a swimming session to be aerobic, you must swim continuously for 30 minutes. That means between 25 and 40 lengths.

This poses two problems. First, you must be a good swimmer (or build up to being one)! Second, you must find a swimming pool that actually allows you to swim. Most people in a pool seem to stand around and splash, and if the pool is busy it is almost impossible to swim lengths. But if you can overcome these obstacles, swimming is a great exercise.

Running

Running can be a beautiful way to exercise, especially on a sunny day in woodland or countryside. It develops high-level stamina. It does, however, demand a reasonable level of fitness just to maintain a steady pace, so for the unfit beginner it is likely to become anaerobic very quickly, even if the pace is slow. If you are unfit, start with a walking program to build up your fitness first.

Whatever your fitness level, the up and down rhythm of running places a considerable strain on the skeletal structure unless proper precautions are taken. These include wearing good quality shoes, avoiding hard roads as much as possible, warming up thoroughly and—most important of all—following the progress principle and building up gradually.

Walking

Walking has many advantages. It is something that, to a greater or lesser extent, we all do already so it does not pose the fear of something new. It does not require any special clothing, so you don't need to feel at all self-conscious. There is little risk of any kind of injury.

But for walking to reach a sufficient intensity and duration to provide real aerobic exercise, it must be brisk and continuous. Even then, it is unlikely to raise most people's pulses beyond the borderline level for quality aerobic exercise. This disadvantage can be counteracted by increasing the duration—walking has to be continued for much longer than other forms of exercise to gain the same effect.

Because walking is a very practical way of getting about, it can often save money and even time. There is no need to walk the whole way if your journey is long, but by parking on the edge of town, or getting off the bus or train one stop earlier, commuters can easily build exercise into their daily routine. At other times, you can increase your enjoyment by choosing a scenic route or by taking children or a dog along.

Cycling

Cycling, like walking, is excellent for beginners and a useful way of getting about. Maximum benefit, however, depends on a steady pedaling rhythm and for this a bicycle with gears is a considerable advantage. Most cyclists pedal too slowly in too high a gear, putting strain on the muscles (developing strength at the expense of stamina) and also increasing the risk of injury. Maximum aerobic benefit as well as efficiency of movement are achieved with a cadence of at least 80 turns of the pedal a minute.

Aerobic Dance

The average aerobics class attempts to combine vigorous aerobic exercise with stretching (suppleness) exercises. It is difficult to provide a series of varied exercises for a class of people at different standards. It is likely to be intense enough to be aerobic for some, but too easy for others. A good warm-up is essential, and you must ensure that the pace of the class is not too fast for your own natural body rhythm. At all costs avoid any fast stretching movements.

If these points are borne in mind, there is no reason not to go ahead. The aim of a good exercise program is enjoyment, and many people love the music and atmosphere of an aerobics class. If the class is led by a qualified and competent instructor and you enjoy it, then it is certainly to be recommended.

Suppleness Sessions

When planning your suppleness session, remember the basic requirements:

1. Go only as far as your body will go without straining. Never bounce, jerk, or force it.
2. Move slowly into each pose, and hold it for five to ten seconds. Then, and not before, try to stretch a little further for another five to ten seconds.
3. Stretch every part of your body, so you are supple all over.

The BLISSS suppleness program that follows allows all these in a very few minutes, so you can easily do it at home on days when you are not busy with your chosen stamina activity.

BELLOWS *Lie on your back. Clasp one knee in both hands and pull it gently into your chest as shown. Repeat with the other knee.*

LATERAL STRETCH *Stand with your feet about 3 feet apart and bend sideways to the position shown. Try to bend from the hips rather than from the ribs and do not lean forward. Repeat on the other side.*

WALL STRETCH *Lean against a wall as shown and, keeping your back leg straight, lower it so your knee moves toward the ground. This stretches your calf muscle. Repeat with the other leg.*

FENCER'S POSE *Stand with your feet 4 to 5 feet apart, with one foot pointing forward and the other sideways. Sink into the position shown so your leading knee is at right angles. Reach out and away from your body with both arms and do not lean forward.*

FORWARD FOLD *Sit with your legs straight in front of you. Keeping your legs and back straight, slide your hands down your legs as far as they will go. Don't worry if you only reach your knees—technique is more important than getting to your ankles.*

COBRA *Lie on your front and raise your upper body into the position shown. This loosens the muscles of your back and stretches your abdominal muscles.*

CAMEL *Kneel on the floor and slowly bend back as far as you can go. It does not matter if you can't reach your ankles.*

THE BOW *Lie on your front. Reach back to grasp your ankles and, by pulling slowly, raise your chest and thighs off the floor.*

Strength Sessions

The following strength exercises are not designed to develop "superstrong" muscles, but to prevent muscle degeneration and correct weaknesses that occur through inactivity or unbalanced exercise. Whereas the stamina exercises involve leg muscles, these exercises provide balance by working on the upper body.

Position 1

Position 2

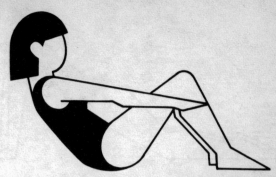

STOMACH *The sit-up is an excellent exercise for the abdominal muscles but it is important to follow the correct technique so that these muscles are used in isolation. First it is necessary to learn the pelvic tilt. From position 1, drop your lower back fully onto the floor by rotating your pelvis upward. Then slowly sit up into position 2 by lifting your head first, followed by your shoulders. Return to position 1 by lowering your lower back first, followed by your shoulders and head. If at first you can't sit up the whole way, don't worry. Just go as far as you can. As you improve, make the exercise harder by clasping your hands behind your head and bending your knees more. Aim for five to 20 repetitions.*

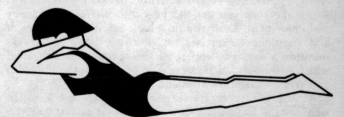

BACK *Balance the sit-up by doing some back raises for your upper and lower back. Lie on your front and, keeping your feet on the floor, slowly raise your upper body as far as it will go comfortably. Then slowly lower it again. Repeat five to 20 times.*

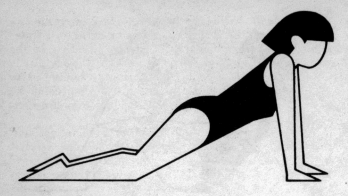

UPPER ARMS AND SHOULDERS *As an introduction to full push-ups start with a modified version. From the position shown bend your arms and lower your upper body until your chest touches the floor, then push up with your arms. Repeat ten to 40 times. When you can do 40 repetitions comfortably, try full push-ups, i.e. raising yourself up on your arms from lying flat on the floor.*

A Final Boost

The BLISSS program has three basic components. First, you raise your base-line level of activity through a whole range of everyday actions, from carrying the shopping to beating an egg. Next, you choose activities to boost your stamina and make sure you get the best from them in efficiency and enjoyment. Last, you do a basic minimum of strength and suppleness exercises on alternate days. So, for 30 minutes a day, you can reach an optimum health level which will do as much as possible to counter the ill health and stress caused by a sedentary life-style.

At the center of the BLISSS concept is the *I* which signifies the individual. You choose what to do, and you feel the benefits. That's why the program includes one day just for "activity sessions".

An activity session is anything you want it to be. It can include activities that contribute nothing toward the three

S factors, but which you happen to find interesting or useful. It might be gardening, chopping wood, or a sport. It might be a trip with family or friends. Children, by the way, are a great help in encouraging activity. They play in a way that creates a great deal of natural exercise! Many adults could learn a lot by joining in with their children's games at *their* level, rather than standing around making suggestions or organizing things.

Whether it's high-level S factor exercise or not, just make sure you do something that reinforces the link between activity and fun. As your fitness improves over the weeks, you will find that your have much more energy and are capable of enjoying activities that were too demanding for you in the past. Take advantage of this and use your activity days to explore new things. All the benefits to your health and your looks will then take on secondary importance—activity and movement will become a joy in themselves. Only then will the BLISS program be achieved and exercise be truly "for life".

12

Choosing Vitamin Supplements

Vitamin supplements can be very beneficial to your health in a stressful twentieth-century life-style. But not all supplements are the same. Analysis of a wide variety of multivitamin tablets to find out how much it would cost to get the basic optimum vitamin requirements produced a range between 20 cents and over five dollars a day! And with so many supplements available, all promising perfect health, it's easy to become confused. For instance, if you're looking for a simple multivitamin preparation to meet the basic optimum requirements, you have over 30 products to choose from.

So picking the right supplements is an art in itself! Unfortunately, not all supplements are true to their labels, so it is not always best to buy the cheapest. Reputable vitamin companies should give you a list of all the ingredients on the label. This chapter will help you through the maze by showing you how to decipher the small print and read between the lines, and how to devise a simple daily routine of vitamin supplements.

Reading the Label

Labeling laws vary from country to country, but many of the same principles stand. Depending on the ingredients, different laws apply and, since these change from time to time, many manufacturers are as confused as members of the public are! Figures 9a and 9b illustrate some of the problems you will confront when setting out to read a label. Figure 9a gives insufficient information, is misleading, shows dosages that are far too low and does not show any vitamins B_6 or D, magnesium, chromium, manganese,

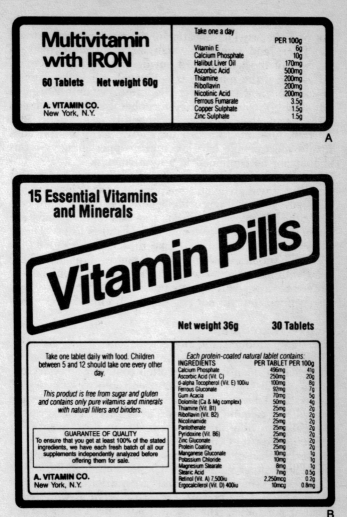

Multivitamin with IRON

60 Tablets   Net weight 60g

A. VITAMIN CO.
New York, N.Y.

Take one a day

	PER 100g
Vitamin E	6g
Calcium Phosphate	10g
Halibut Liver Oil	170mg
Ascorbic Acid	500mg
Thiamine	200mg
Riboflavin	200mg
Nicotinic Acid	200mg
Ferrous Fumarate	3.5g
Copper Sulphate	1.5g
Zinc Sulphate	1.5g

A

15 Essential Vitamins and Minerals

Vitamin Pills

Net weight 36g   30 Tablets

Take one tablet daily with food. Children between 5 and 12 should take one every other day.

This product is free from sugar and gluten and contains only pure vitamins and minerals with natural fillers and binders.

GUARANTEE OF QUALITY
To ensure that you get at least 100% of the stated ingredients, we have each fresh batch of all our supplements independently analyzed before offering them for sale.

A. VITAMIN CO.
New York, N.Y.

Each protein-coated natural tablet contains:

INGREDIENTS	PER TABLET	PER 100g
Calcium Phosphate	496mg	41g
Ascorbic Acid (Vit. C)	250mg	20g
d-alpha Tocopherol (Vit. E) 100iu	100mg	8g
Ferrous Gluconate	92mg	7g
Gum Acacia	70mg	5g
Dolomite (Ca & Mg complex)	50mg	4g
Thiamine (Vit. B1)	25mg	2g
Riboflavin (Vit. B2)	25mg	2g
Nicotinamide	25mg	2g
Pantothenate	25mg	2g
Pyridoxine (Vit. B6)	25mg	2g
Zinc Gluconate	25mg	2g
Protein Coating	25mg	2g
Manganese Gluconate	10mg	1g
Potassium Chloride	10mg	1g
Magnesium Stearate	8mg	1g
Stearic Acid	7mg	0.5g
Retinol (Vit. A) 7,500iu	2,250mcg	0.2g
Ergocalciterol (Vit. D) 400iu	10mcg	0.8mg

B

Figure 9 What to look out for in multivitamin tablets. A. Confusing and lacking sufficient information; a poor nutrient formula B. Accurate and informative; a good nutrient formula

or selenium. The words used in the list of ingredients do not provide easy identification of the nutrients present and the fillers and binders—which make up more than 75 percent of the tablets—are not described. The "elemental" value of the minerals is not stated; nor is the amount of each nutrient per tablet. The form of vitamin E used is not stated: it could be mixed tocopherols, which are much less potent than D-alpha tocopherols (see Figure 9b). Ferrous fumarate can can be a toxic form of iron and, finally, most people have too much copper already, so this should not be contained in a multivitamin.

You ought not to find a multivitamin label as bad as this one! But it will give you some idea of what to look out for. Compare it with Figure 9b, where the dosages are correct, the chemical names for the different vitamins are given, and the filler (calcium phosphate) is listed. Directions for when and how to take the tablets are given, as well as extra information and a guarantee of quality. These are the things to go for when you are buying supplements: do not be misled by an attractive-looking label or a very cheap price, but do not pay too much either!

Active Ingredients

For some products the ingredients have to be listed in order of weight, starting with the ingredient present in the greatest quantity. This is often confusing since included in this list are the non-nutrient additives needed to make the tablet. For instance, in Figure 9b the first ingredient, calcium phosphate, is a "filler". In this case it does also provide nutritional benefit, so it is a good filler substance to use. Often the chemical name of the nutrient is used instead of the common vitamin code (for example, ergocalciferol for vitamin D). These names are all listed in Chapter 13. Since multivitamins are nutrients, the amount of each ingredient per 100g must be listed as well as the amount per tablet. This law was introduced so that when you eat 100g of a cereal, for example, you know how many vitamins you're getting.

The most confusing labels of all may give you only information like:

Cod Liver Oil tablets (750 capsules) Net Weight: 150g
Ingredients per 100g: Retinol 516mg

To find out how much vitamin A you would be getting you
have to be a mathematician! If 750 capsules weigh 150g,
100g is equivalent to 500 capsules. Since 500 capsules
therefore contain 516mg, each capsule contains 1.032mg
or 1,032mcg of retinol (vitamin A). Converted to International Units (1 IU = 0.34mcg) that's 3,000 IU per capsule.
Good vitamin companies keep you better informed than
this.

Fillers and Binders

Not all products have to declare the other ingredients
included in the supplement for manufacturing reasons.
Tablets start off as powders. To get the bulk right "fillers"
are added. "Binders" are added to give the mixture the
right consistency and lubricants are also used. Only when
this is done can the mixture be turned into small, uneven
granules, which are then pressed into tablets under considerable force. Granulating allows the mixture to lock
together, forming a solid mass. The tablet is then coated
with a "protein coating" to protect it from deterioration
and make it easier to swallow.

Unfortunately, many tablets also have coloring and flavoring added, as well as a sugar coating. For instance,
many vitamin C tablets are made to look orange and taste
sweet, since we associate vitamin C with oranges! Vitamin
C is naturally almost white and certainly isn't sweet—and
nor should your supplement be. As a rule of thumb, only
buy supplements that declare their fillers and binders
(sometimes also called "excipients"). Companies with in-
tegrity are usually only too happy to display this information. The following fillers and binders are fine to use and
some add extra nutritious properties to the tablet:

Dicalcium phosphate—a natural filler providing calcium
and phosphate
Cellulose—a natural binder consisting of plant fiber
Alginic acid/sodium alginate—a natural binder from
seaweed

Gum acacia/gum arabic—a natural vegetable gum
Calcium or magnesium stearate—a natural lubricant
Silica—a natural lubricant
Zein—a corn protein for coating the tablet
Brazil wax—a natural coating from palm trees

Many of the better tablets will also declare that the
product is free from sugar and gluten. If you are allergic to
milk or yeast do check that the tablets are also free from
lactose (milk sugar) and yeast. Many B vitamins are derived from yeast, so you need to be careful. If in doubt,
contact the company and ask for an independent "assay" of
the ingredients: good companies will supply this information. Sometimes glucose, fructose, or dextrose is used to
sweeten a tablet and yet the tablet still declares "no
sugar". These are best avoided. A small amount of fructose
is the least evil if you're having difficulty enticing a child
to take vitamins. Any other preservatives or flavoring agents
should be avoided unless they are natural. For instance,
pineapple essence is a natural additive.

Capsules Versus Tablets
Capsules are made of gelatin, which is an animal product
and therefore not suitable for vegetarians. Many capsules
also contain a preservative called methyl paraben, which
stops the gelatin decaying or dissolving. In some countries
this is banned although the law is rarely enforced. I prefer
not to take such preservatives and therefore avoid capsules. Most vitamins can be provided as tablets. For
instance, natural vitamin E comes in two forms: D-alpha
tocopherol acetate (oil) or D-alpha tocopherol succinate
(powder). Both are equally potent.

Natural Versus Synthetic
A great deal of misleading information has been said and
written about the advantages of natural vitamins. First of
all, many products claiming to be natural simply aren't. By
law, a certain percentage of a product must be natural for
the product to be declared "natural". The percentage
varies from country to country. By careful wording some

supplements sound natural but really aren't. For instance, "vitamin C with rosehips" invariably means synthetic vitamin C with added rosehips, although it is often confused with vitamin C *from* rosehips. So which is better?

By definition, a synthetic vitamin must contain *all* the properties of the vitamin found in nature. If it doesn't then the chemists haven't done their job properly. This is the case with vitamin E. Natural D-alpha tocopherol succinate is 36 percent more potent than the synthetic vitamin E called Dl-alpha tocopherol (in this case the *l* dictates the chemical difference). So natural vitamin E, usually derived from wheat germ or soy oil, is better.

However, synthetic vitamin C (ascorbic acid) has the same biological potency as the natural substance, according to Dr. Linus Pauling,[1] although chromatography and Kirlian photography have shown visible differences between the two.[2] No one has yet shown that natural vitamin C is more potent or beneficial to take. Indeed, most vitamin C is synthesized by taking a "natural" sugar, such as dextrose; two chemical reactions later you have ascorbic acid. This is little different from the chemical reactions that take place in animals that convert sugar to vitamin C. Vitamin C derived from, say, acerola cherries—the most concentrated source—is also considerably bulkier and more expensive. Acerola is only 20 percent vitamin C, so a 1,000mg tablet would be five times as large as a normal tablet and would cost you ten times as much![3]

It is true that vitamins derived from natural sources may contain an unknown element that increases their potency. With vitamin E this may well be octacosanol, a nutritional substance found in vegetable oils. Vitamin C is found in nature together with the bioflavanoids, active nutrients that appear to increase the potency of vitamin C, particularly in its capacity of strengthening the capillaries or tiny blood vessels. The best source of bioflavanoids is citrus fruit, so the addition of citrus bioflavanoids to vitamin C tablets is one step closer to nature.

It is possible that yeast and rice bran, which are excellent sources of B vitamins, also contain unknown beneficial ingredients, so these vitamins are best supplied with yeast or rice bran. Brewer's yeast tablets or powder are far less efficient ways of taking B vitamins than B Complex vitamin supplements with a little added yeast—one would have to eat pounds of yeast tablets to get optimum levels of B vitamins. However, watch out for yeast. Some people are allergic to it and if you react badly to any vitamin supplements it could be yeast causing the problem.

Elemental Minerals

Minerals in multivitamin and mineral tablets often omit the "elemental" value of the compound, stating only the amount of the mineral compound. For instance, 100mg of zinc gluconate or zinc orotate will provide only 10mg of zinc and 90mg of orotic acid (sometimes called vitamin B_{13}). Since it's the mineral you're after, check the figures carefully. If your supplement says "zinc gluconate (providing 5mg zinc) 50mg" you're getting 5mg of zinc. Otherwise, you may have to contact the manufacturer for more detailed information. Most good companies declare this information either on the label or in literature that comes with the product.

When a mineral is attached to a compound such as an amino acid it is called "chelated", from the Greek word for a claw. Chelated minerals are often absorbed twice as well and, in a sense, mimic what the body does normally.[4] When we ingest a mineral it is normally combined with an amino acid, a constituent of protein, to be absorbed. So minerals normally have to compete for amino acids—and not all of them win. Zinc, for instance, has to compete with lead for the same chelating agents. By providing already chelated minerals absorption is far better.

What Is Sustained Release?

Some vitamins are called prolonged, sustained, or time released, implying that the ingredients are not all made available for absorption in one go. This can be useful when taking large amounts of water-soluble vitamins such as B Complex or vitamin C. However, absorption depends also on the person and on the dosage. Some people are able to absorb and use 1,000mg of vitamin C taken in one dose;

taking it in sustained release form would provide little benefit. However, if you take three 1,000mg tablets each day, sustained release would allow you to take them all in one go. Since sustained release vitamins are more expensive one has to weigh up the pros and cons. There is no point in having a sustained release fat-soluble vitamin, such as vitamins A, D, or E, as these can be stored in the body.

Which Supplements Are Good Value?

For a supplement to be good value it must be well made, well formulated, and well priced. The quality of manufacture is hard to assess unless you have an advanced chemistry laboratory in your back room! However, there are three simple tests you can do:

1. Are the stated number of tablets actually in the bottle? (We tested one company and found an average of 95 tablets instead of 100!)
2. Is the tablet coated all round and therefore easy to swallow? (Uncoated or badly coated tablets can break up or taste unpleasant.)
3. Does the label tell you everything you need to know? (The better the company the more information they will want to give you.)

Ideal Formulas

Every nutritionist has different ideas about the "best" blend of vitamins and minerals in supplements, and this is reflected in the ever-growing range to choose from. The ideal formulation ultimately depends on your needs, but there are certain basic ones that act as building blocks for your personal health program. These are a B Complex, a multivitamin, a multimineral, and a vitamin C tablet. These recommended formulas will cover the basic nutrient requirements for optimum health. Depending on your signs of deficiency you may also need to add extra B vitamins or individual minerals.

B COMPLEX This should contain at least 25mg each of B_1, B_2, PABA, choline, and inositol, and 50mg of B_3, B_5, and B_6, as well as 10mcg of B_{12}, 50mcg of folic acid and 50mcg of biotin.

MULTIVITAMIN This should contain 7,500 IU of A, 400 IU of D, 100 IU of E, 250mg of C, and 25mg of B_1, B_2, B_3, B_5, and B_6. (If it is to be taken on its own as a complete multivitamin and mineral, extra B_{12}, folic acid, biotin, PABA, choline, inositol, and minerals are needed, as well as more vitamin C.) Often calcium, magnesium, iron, zinc, and manganese are included as these are frequently deficient.

MULTIMINERAL This should provide 150mg of calcium, 75 mg of magnesium, 10mg of iron, 10mg of zinc, 2.5mg of manganese, 20mcg of chromium, and 25mcg of selenium. (Selenium is often excluded as it is better absorbed on an empty stomach.)

VITAMIN C This should provide 1,000mg of vitamin C with at least 25mg of bioflavanoids.

How to Turn Your Nutrient Needs into a Simple Supplement Program

From your scores in the checklists in Chapter 9, you will have worked out your optimum daily nutrient needs. If you scored less than five on each vitamin and mineral your needs are easily covered by this program:

SUPPLEMENT	DAILY
B Complex	1
Multivitamin	1
Multimineral	1
Vitamin C 1,000mg	1

If you scored five or more for vitamins A, D, or E, you'll need to double the multivitamin. A score of seven or more on vitamin E will warrant a separate vitamin E supplement. If you scored seven or more on at least two B vitamins your best bet is to take two B Complex tablets per day. However, if you only scored high on B_6, for example, adding a B_6 supplement of the desired strength will be more practical. The same applied to vitamin C. If your optimum level is 2,000mg take two vitamin C tablets per day.

If you scored five or more for at least two minerals, double your multimineral intake. However, if only calcium and magnesium were deficient, these can be provided together in dolomite, a natural form of calcium and magnesium. If you are especially in need of chromium you may also require extra vitamin B_3, so some manufacturers combine the two. The same is true to zinc, and B_6,[5] so look out for these combined nutrients since they will save you money and decrease the number of tablets you take. Selenium is much better absorbed without food,[6] and some manufacturers therefore leave it out of their combined formulas. Those particularly low in selenium may therefore wish to take a selenium supplement separately.

When Should You Take Vitamin Supplements?

Now that you've worked out what to take, you'll want to know when to take them. This depends not only on what is technically best, but also on your life-style. If taking supplements twice a day would mean that you'd forget the second lot, you're probably best advised to take them all at once! After all, nature supplies them in one go, with a meal. Here are the "ten commandments" of supplement taking:

1. Take vitamins and minerals 15 minutes before or after, or during a meal.
2. Selenium is better absorbed on an empty stomach— try first thing in the morning.
3. Don't take B vitamins late at night if you have difficulty sleeping.
4. Take multiminerals or dolomite tablets in the evening— these help you to sleep.

5. If you're taking two or more B Complex or vitamin Cs take one at each meal.
6. If you are anemic (iron deficient) take extra iron with vitamin C. Avoid "ferric" forms of iron.
7. If you are zinc deficient take extra zinc with vitamin B_6.
8. If you know you are copper deficient take copper only with 16 times as much zinc, e.g. 0.5mg copper to 8mg zinc.
9. If you are taking Glucomannan take most of your vitamin supplements with breakfast and most of your Glucomannan with lunch or dinner.
10. Always take your supplements. Irregular supplementation doesn't work.

What Improvements in Health Can I Expect?

Vitamins and minerals are not drugs, so you shouldn't expect an overnight improvement in your health. Most people on personal health programs have experienced definite improvement in health within three months. This is the shortest length of time that you should experiment with a program. The earliest noticeable health changes are increased energy, more emotional stability, and improvements in the condition of hair and skin. Your health will continue to improve as long as you are following the right program. My health is still improving after five years! If you do not experience any noticeable improvement in three months, it is best to see a nutrition consultant.

How Often Should I Reassess My Needs?

Certainly at the beginning your needs will change and a reassessment every three months is sensible. Your nutrient needs should decrease as you get healthier. Remember, you need optimum nutrition most when you are stressed. So when the emergencies occur, or you're working especially hard, make doubly sure that you eat well and take your supplements every day.

Are There Any Side Effects?

Nutrients are not drugs, so there can be no serious side effects. However, you may find that your bowels will be looser if you are taking 1,000mg to 3,000mg of vitamin C, and your urine will become yellower as a result of B_2 (riboflavin). Vitamin B_3 in the form of niacin is a vasodilator. This means that your capillaries dilate, causing a "blushing" sensation. It can be quite pronounced and, although good for you, not everybody likes it. So proceed with caution. 100mg of B_3 is enough to cause this effect.

Can Vitamins Be Dangerous?

All food substances are toxic if taken in excess; vitamins and minerals are no exception. However, the fact that vitamins can be toxic in large doses has been exploited. For instance, a recent article reporting toxicity of vitamin B_6 at levels of 2,000mg to 6,000mg per day—at least eight times greater than the *maximum* optimum level suggested!—was recently used as ammunition to ban high-dose B_6 supplements.[7,8] The toxic vitamin is vitamin A, which can cause death at levels of 1,000,000 IU in one dose.[9] With the highest supplement containing 7,500 IU per tablet, you would have to take 134 tablets in one go to kill yourself! However, care should be taken with this vitamin as it can be stored in the liver and can accumulate there if massive doses are taken.

Table 7 lists the minimum levels of each vitamin found to be toxic. However, since toxicity of some vitamins has not been thoroughly researched it is far better to err on the side of caution. Provided you do not exceed the maximum levels recommended in the optimum range given in Chapter 13 you are more than safe.

Children are more susceptible to vitamin toxicity and for children the recommended levels should be reduced according to body weight. For example, a 70lb child should certainly never take more than 10,000 IU of vitamin A. Some recent animal research suggests that extremely large amounts of vitamin A can interfere with fetal development, therefore pregnant women should not exceed 10,000 IU of vitamin A unless recommended to do so by a nutritionally-oriented doctor or a nutrition consultant. Vitamin A in the form of beta-carotene has not been shown to be toxic.

Toxic Level of Vitamins and Minerals		
Nutrient	Toxic Level (lowest level at which symptoms are reported)	Maximum Level Recommended (for those with severe deficiency)
Vitamin A(Retinol)	200,000 IU [10,11]	20,000 IU
Vitamin A(Beta carotene)	none found[12,13]	20,000 IU
Vitamin D	100,000 IU[14]	1,000 IU
Vitamin E	800[15] to 1,600 IU[16]	1,000 IU
Vitamin B$_1$ (Thiamine)	none found[17]	100mg
Vitamin B$_2$ (Riboflavin)	none found[18]	100mg
Vitamin B$_3$(Niacin)	3,000 to 10,000mg[19]	150mg
Vitamin B$_3$ (Nicotinamide)	3,000 to 10,000mg[20]	150mg
Vitamin B$_5$ (Pantothenic acid)	none found[21]	300mg
Vitamin B$_6$ (Pyridoxine)	2,000mg[22]	250mg
Vitamin B$_{12}$	none found[23]	100mcg
Folic acid	none found[23]	400mcg
PABA	none found[23]	150mg
Choline	none found[23]	150mg
Inositol	none found[23]	150mg
Vitamin C	10,000mg + [24]	4,000mg

Table 7

Vitamin E in amounts greater than 100 IU should not be taken by those with rheumatic fever or high blood pressure without supervision. Although vitamin E is especially beneficial for those with cardiovascular problems, the dosage should be increased gradually. A sudden increase of vitamin E can cause the heart to pump more efficiently— in those with a poor circulatory condition this can result in too rapid a heartbeat. If in doubt it is always best to ask your doctor.

Provided you follow these guidelines, vitamins are almost as nontoxic as water. I have only seen one mild case of vitamin toxicity in 2,000 patients. Most of the others were deficient!

Vitamins Versus Drugs

Many medical drugs cause vitamin losses and increase the chance of vitamin deficiency. For this reason it is often doubly important that you do ensure adequate vitamin status if you are receiving medication. For instance, if you take antibiotics it is wise to add an extra B Complex supplement to your program. However, there are a few medical drugs that cause so much interference that it is unwise to take vitamins with them in particular forms. Among them are the MAOIs (mono-amine oxidase inhibitors), which are antidepressants. Yeast and vitamin B_6 are not recommended when taking these. If in doubt always ask your doctor.

13

A–Z of Vitamins

Vitamin A

Vitamin A is a fat-soluble vitamin, supplied to us in fats and oils. As a supplement it is best taken with a meal. Vitamin A from animals is called retinol and is twice as potent as vitamin A from vegetables, called beta carotene. It is measured in IU or mcg. 0.3mcg of retinol = 0.6mcg beta carotene = 1 IU of vitamin A.

WHAT IT DOES Vitamin A is essential for healthy eyesight and night vision, which is why carrots really do help you see in the dark. It also strengthens your skin, inside and out, protecting mucous membranes like the lungs and digestive tract from infection and damage. For this reason, it protects against aging, cancer, bronchitis, ulcers, and skin conditions like acne and eczema. It is also needed to make sex hormones and protein.

SIGNS OF DEFICIENCY Poor night vision, low resistance to infection, dry flaky skin, dandruff, some forms of acne, frequent mouth ulcers, loss of appetite, headaches, and nausea. [1, 2]

WHERE TO FIND IT Most of your vitamin A is supplied from animal sources. It is highest in the liver, which is why cod liver oil is often given as a nutrient. It is added to margarine, and is present in dairy produce and eggs. Beta carotene, the vegetable form, is especially high in yellow/red vegetables such as carrots and beets, and is also found in green leafy vegetables, such as broccoli and spinach.

HOW MUCH DO YOU NEED? Vitamin A is stored in the liver so you don't have to take it every day. In some countries where deficiency is common 200,000 IU are given twice a year. Infectious diseases put up your needs. Individuals' needs can vary by up to a five-fold factor, so it is essential to monitor signs of deficiency in order to estimate your requirements. Some animal research has shown large amounts of vitamin A to cause birth defects,[3] so women wanting to become pregnant are advised not to take more than 10,000 IU or 20,000 IU daily if they have symptoms of deficiency.

RDA: 3,300 IU (USA);[4] 2,500 IU (UK & Australia)

Optimum range for adults: 7,500 IU to 20,000 IU

Optimum range for children (aged three to 12): 3,750 IU to 10,000 IU

Single dose toxic level 800,000 IU[5]

Continuous dose toxic level (over three months): 200,000 IU[5]

SUPPLEMENTS Fish liver oil or beta carotene are good sources. Beta carotene is to be preferred when doses in excess of 50,000 IU are used for long periods of time, since this form has no known toxicity.[6]

FRIENDS Vitamin A cannot work properly in the body without zinc.[7] Vitamins C and E help protect vitamin A in the body. Vitamin D is usually supplied with A since they occur together in nature.

ENEMIES A is destroyed by heat, light, and by excesses of iron or copper in cooking vessels.

B Complex

The term B Complex describes a group of vitamins including thiamine (B_1), riboflavin (B_2), niacin or nicotinic acid (B_3), pantothenic acid (B_5), pyridoxine (B_6), cyanocobalamine (B_{12}), folic acid, and biotin. Some authorities also include PABA (para-amino-benzoic-acid), choline, and inositol. These vitamins tend to occur together in nature and have many similar functions. Since they are all water-soluble, they need to be supplied on a daily basis as little gets stored in the body.

WHAT THEY DO Individual B vitamins have different roles to play in keeping us healthy. Together they keep us mentally alert and emotionally stable, they improve our energy and ability to deal with stress, and they have positive effects on our hair and skin. B vitamins are also essential for a good circulation system, the correct balance of hormones, and a strong immune system to protect us from infections.

SIGNS OF DEFICIENCY Confusion, irritability, depression, insomnia, tension, difficulty relaxing, poor memory, hair loss, premature grey hair, bad skin, poor appetite, neuritis, constipation, sleepiness after meals, allergies, hay fever, low energy, and poor stamina.

WHERE TO FIND THEM The best sources are wholegrains, seeds, nuts, vegetables, beans, lentils, yeast, molasses, eggs, and milk products.

HOW MUCH DO YOU NEED? Individual needs vary enormously and are very dependent on how active you are.

Vitamin B₁

Vitamin B_1 is called thiamine and was discovered in 1926 to be the factor that stopped beri-beri, a disease of the nervous system.

WHAT IT DOES It is needed to turn glucose into energy for the muscles and the nervous system and is also involved in the production of acetylcholine, the body's major nerve-transmitter. It is also involved in protein metabolism. Deficiency of thiamine affects digestion as well as energy and nerve transmission.

SIGNS OF DEFICIENCY Tender muscles, stomach pains, constipation, prickly sensations in the legs, eye pains, loss of weight, mental confusion.[8]

WHERE TO FIND IT See B Complex.

HOW MUCH DO YOU NEED? Deficiency occurs primarily among those who eat refined grains, like white rice or white flour—for this reason, white flour is now fortified with thiamine. Greater levels of B_1 are needed by those whose diets are high in carbohydrates. Alcohol destroys B_1 so the more you drink, the more you need.[9]
RDA: 1.4mg (USA)[4]; 1.1mg (UK & Australia); 1.2mg (New Zealand)[4]
Optimum range for adults: 25mg to 100mg
Optimum range for children (aged three to 12): 12.5mg to 50mg
Toxic level: none known[5]

SUPPLEMENTS Thiamine is provided as thiamine hydrochloride or thiamine nitrate, both of which are fine sources.

FRIENDS Thiamine interacts with other B vitamins as well as manganese.

ENEMIES It is destroyed by alcohol, alkaline agents such as baking powder, and sulphur dioxide which is used as a preservative. Some 30 to 40 percent also leaches out of foods in cooking.

Vitamin B_2
Riboflavin (vitamin B_2) is almost fluorescent yellow in color. When sufficient amounts are taken it will color the urine, but the effect is quite harmless.

WHAT IT DOES It is essential for manufacturing enzymes that convert protein, fats, and carbohydrates into energy. Normal growth and cellular repair also depend on riboflavin, and it helps to regulate acidity in the body.

SIGNS OF DEFICIENCY Bloodshot itchy eyes, burning or "gritty" eyes, sore tongue, cracked lips, cataracts, eczema, dull oily hair, split nails, trembling, sluggishness, dizziness, sores around the mouth and eyes, and sensitivity to light.[10]

WHERE TO FIND IT See B Complex. B_2 is easily destroyed by light and therefore milk, which may be exposed to sunlight, is not such a good supply.

HOW MUCH DO YOU NEED? There is some evidence to suggest that fetuses are susceptible to B_2 deficiency, so pregnant mothers need more. Alcohol, cigarettes, and the birth control pill all increase the need for this vitamin.
RDA: 1.6mg (USA); 1.7mg (UK & New Zealand)[4]; 1.4mg (Australia)
Optimum range for adults: 25mg to 100mg
Optimum range for children (aged three to 12): 12.5mg to 50mg
Toxic level: none known

SUPPLEMENTS Riboflavin supplements above 25mg will color the urine.

FRIENDS B_2 should be taken with other B vitamins.

ENEMIES Heat, ultraviolet light, alkaline solutions, and leaching when food is cooked.

Vitamin B_3

Vitamin B_3 has four names depending on which side of the Atlantic you live. In the USA it is called niacin or niacinamide. In Britain it is called nicotinic acid or nicotinamide. Niacin/nicotinic acid causes a blushing effect by dilating the capillaries. Niacinamide does not cause this effect. Both can be used; niacin is more effective at lowering high cholesterol levels.

WHAT IT DOES First noticed for its effect on the mental illness pellagra, B_3 is crucial for proper function of the brain, where it helps to make a number of chemicals, including serotonin which is involved with sleep. It is essential for energy production and helps maintain healthy skin. B_3 is contained in GTF, the glucose tolerance factor, which helps maintain normal blood sugar levels.

SIGNS OF DEFICIENCY Fatigue, depression, rapid mood swings, fearfulness, headaches, loss of appetite, migraines, bad breath, acne, rough inflamed skin, coated tongue, tremors, loss of memory, insomnia, and allergies.

WHERE TO FIND IT See B Complex. However, B_3 can also be made from the protein constituent tryptophan, so foods high in tryptophan, such as chicken, contribute to your B_3 status. 60mg of tryptophan make 1mg of B_3.

HOW MUCH DO YOU NEED? Individual needs vary considerably. High carbohydrate diets call for more B_3. For most people, the blushing effect occurs when 100mg of niacin is taken.
RDA: 18mg (USA & UK)[4]
Optimum range for adults: 50mg to 150mg
Optimum range for children (aged three to 12): 25mg to 75mg
Single dose toxic level: 3,000mg[5]

SUPPLEMENTS Use half niacin and half niacinamide, since the blushing effect is beneficial, unless you dislike the effect in which case use niacinamide alone.

FRIENDS Chromium and B_3 are needed to make GTF; these two should be supplied together for those with poor glucose tolerance. B_6 is needed to convert tryptophan to B_3.

ENEMIES B_3 is very stable, although leaching during cooking and destruction by alcohol does occur.

Vitamin B$_5$

Vitamin B$_5$ is called pantothenic acid, derived from the Greek word *panthos,* meaning everywhere, because it is found in so many foods.

WHAT IT DOES Pantothenic acid is essential for energy production and helps make antistress hormones. It also helps make acetylcholine, which is an important nerve-transmitter substance. It has been successfully used in the the treatment of arthritic diseases.[12]

SIGNS OF DEFICIENCY Poor concentration, apathy, restlessness, vomiting, asthma, allergies, burning feet, muscle cramps, and exhaustion.

WHERE TO FIND IT It is particularly high in eggs, chicken, fish, molasses, and brewer's yeast, although it is also found in numerous other foods.

HOW MUCH DO YOU NEED? Little is known about the causes for individual variation in requirements. Under conditions of stress B$_5$ needs increase considerably.
RDA: not established
Optimum range for adults: 50mg to 300mg
Optimum range for children (aged three to 12): 25mg to 150mg
Toxic level: none known

SUPPLEMENTS Calcium pantothenate is the common type of B$_5$ used in supplements.

FRIENDS Biotin and folic acid help the absorption of B$_5$. It is best taken with other B vitamins.

ENEMIES It is destroyed by heat, food processing, and extremes of acidity and alkalinity, such as in vinegar or baking powder.

Vitamin B$_6$

Called pyridoxine, vitamin B$_6$ is one of the most frequently deficient B vitamins. Minimum RDAs are about 2mg, but 100mg is needed for premenstrual problems, so the individual variation in needs is large. Women tend to need more than men.

WHAT IT DOES It is needed to convert tryptophan into B_3, so B_6 deficiency can also result in B_3 deficiency. It helps make certain brain chemicals—an excess of B_6 causes vivid dreams and restlessness. It also helps make enzymes involved with the breakdown of fats, carbohydrates, and protein.

SIGNS OF DEFICIENCY Irritability, depression, bloatedness and water retention, loss of hair, numbness, muscle cramps, slow learning, pregnancy sickness or depression, allergies, tingling hands, menopausal arthritis, poor dream recall and memory.[13]

WHERE TO FIND IT See B Complex.

HOW MUCH DO YOU NEED? High levels of estrogen hormone increase the need for this vitamin, so more is needed prior to menstruation and for those on the birth control pill. A high protein diet also calls for more B_6.[14]
RDA: 2mg (USA & New Zealand); 1.5mg (Australia); (UK none established)[4]
Optimum range for adults: 50mg to 250mg
Optimum range for children (aged three to 12): 25mg to 125mg
Toxic level: 2,000mg[15]

SUPPLEMENTS B_6 supplements are best taken with zinc since a number of B_6's functions are dependent on zinc.

FRIENDS zinc, B_3, magnesium, and other B vitamins.

ENEMIES Copper, alcohol, smoking, and certain drugs (isoniazid, hydralazine, penicillamine), including the birth control pill.

Vitamin B$_{12}$

Vitamin B$_{12}$ called cyanocobalamine is known as the antipernicious anemia factor. It is the only vitamin that contains a mineral, cobalt, hence its name. To be used by the body it requires the presence of "intrinsic factor", which is normally produced in the stomach.

WHAT IT DOES It is essential for the production of red blood cells, which carry oxygen, and is also needed to make DNA. B$_{12}$ helps make the myelin sheath that insulates nerves.

SIGNS OF DEFICIENCY Anemia, smooth and sore tongue, tremors, lassitude, menstrual problems, mental disorders.[16]

WHERE TO FIND IT B$_{12}$ is found in all animal produce such as meat, eggs, and milk, but is scarce in the vegetable kingdom. It is found in comfrey and also in large amounts in spirulina, a form of algae.

HOW MUCH DO YOU NEED? Vegetarians are advised to take extra, since very little is supplied through their diet. The major problem is usually one of absorption—only 1 percent of dietary intake is absorbed and therefore pernicious anemia is treated by injection.
RDA: 3mcg (USA & New Zealand); 2mcg (Australia); (UK none established)[4]
Optimum range for adults: 5mcg to 100mcg
Optimum range for children (aged three to 12): 2.5mcg to 50 mcg
Toxic level: none known

SUPPLEMENTS B$_{12}$ is supplied as cyanocobalamine; there is no evidence that extra intake of cobalt affects B$_{12}$ status.

FRIENDS A small amount of calcium is needed for absorption.

ENEMIES Any problems of absorption; also alcohol.

Folic Acid

As with vitamin B_{12}, anemia will result when folic acid is low. The amount of folic acid available for sale is restricted, since taking it can mask B_{12} deficiency anemia, although the nerve degeneration that occurs with B_{12} deficiency would still occur. Recently, insufficient folic acid has been associated with spina bifida, a neural tube defect, in fetuses.

WHAT IT DOES It is needed to make RNA and DNA and is therefore essential for the manufacture and repair of all cells. It also helps to regulate histamine levels in the body.[17]

SIGNS OF DEFICIENCY Anemia, weakness, fatigue, breathlessness, and certain symptoms of mental illness.[18]

WHERE TO FIND IT See B Complex.

HOW MUCH DO YOU NEED? Much more is needed during pregnancy, especially for those who have previously had a miscarriage.
RDA: none established
Optimum range for adults: 50mcg to 400mcg
Optimum range for children (aged three to 12): 25mg to 200mg
Toxic level: none known

SUPPLEMENTS Folic acid should not be taken without a basic intake of B_{12}.

FRIENDS Vitamin C helps utilize folic acid and prevent its destruction.

ENEMIES High temperatures and light can destroy this vitamin.

Biotin

Biotin is a rather ignored B vitamin, which was discovered when consumption of a raw egg white resulted in illness.

Avidin, a protein in egg that is destroyed by cooking, induces biotin deficiency.

WHAT IT DOES It is involved in the metabolism of proteins, fats, and carbohydrates. It helps maintain healthy skin, hair, and a balanced hormonal system.

SIGNS OF DEFICIENCY These are rare but do sometimes occur in babies: anemia, dermatitis, scaly skin, and diarrhea.[19]

WHERE TO FIND IT See B Complex. Biotin is high in milk produce, and a large amount is produced in the intestine when the right bacteria are present.

HOW MUCH DO YOU NEED? Not really established, although daily intake is around 150mcg to 300mcg.
RDA: none established
Optimum range for adults: 50mcg to 200mcg
Optimum range for children (aged three to 12): 25mcg to 100mcg
Toxic level: none known

SUPPLEMENTS Biotin should be supplied in your B Complex or multivitamin preparation.

FRIENDS None known as such; it is best taken with other B vitamins.

ENEMIES Raw egg white.

PABA (para-amino-benzoic-acid)
The role of PABA in the body is not well understood.

WHAT IT DOES It is needed for healthy skin and hair growth, with a particular function in skin pigmentation. It is a very effective sunscreen and is used to treat vitiligo, a condition in which parts of the skin lose their color. It prevents grey hair in some animals.

SIGNS OF DEFICIENCY None well established—possibly poor tanning ability.

WHERE TO FIND IT See B Complex.

HOW MUCH DO YOU NEED? Not known for certain.
RDA: none established
Optimum range for adults: 25mg to 150mg
Optimum range for children (aged three to 12): 12.5mg to 75mg
Toxic level: none known

SUPPLEMENTS PABA should be supplied in your B Complex or multivitamin formula.

FRIENDS Folic acid.

ENEMIES Sulphonamide drugs—PABA should not be used when these are being taken.

Choline
Choline is a constituent of lecithin and can be made by the body so, strictly speaking, it is not a vitamin.

WHAT IS DOES It helps make acetylcholine and is essential for brain function. In large amounts choline improves memory and mental function.[20] As a constituent of lecithin it helps to break down accumulating fats in the liver.

SIGNS OF DEFICIENCY Signs of circulatory disease, such as high blood pressure or excess cholesterol, may be partly due to choline deficiency.

WHERE TO FIND IT Choline is high in fish, eggs, and lecithin.

HOW MUCH DO YOU NEED? People with circulatory problems or senile dementia are advised to take more.
RDA: None established
Optimum range for adults: 25mg to 150mg
Optimum range for children (aged three to 12): 12.5mg to 75mg
Toxic level: none known

SUPPLEMENTS Choline can be taken in the form of lecithin, choline bitartrate, or phosphatidyl choline. Choline chloride has the unfortunate side effect of leaving you smelling like dead fish!

FRIENDS Vitamin B_5.

ENEMIES Alcohol.

Inositol

Inositol, also a constituent of lecithin, is again not strictly a vitamin since it can be made by the body.

WHAT IT DOES Its exact function is not known but it is found in large quantities in the nerves and is thought to have a mild tranquilizing effect in large doses.

SIGNS OF DEFICIENCY None have been established.

WHERE TO FIND IT The same as for choline.

HOW MUCH DO YOU NEED? Not known. Doses of 1,000mg a day are said to have a mild tranquilizing effect,[21] though this has not been confirmed by all researchers.
RDA: none established
Optimum range for adults: 25mg to 150mg
Optimum range for children (aged three to 12): 12.5mg to 75mg
Toxic level: none known

SUPPLEMENTS Inositol can be taken in lecithin or by itself. It is usually found in B Complex tablets.

FRIENDS Choline.

ENEMIES None known.

Vitamin C

Vitamin C, perhaps the best known vitamin, may in fact
not be a vitamin at all. All animals, except guinea pigs,
monkeys, and fruit bats, can produce their own vitamin C
from glucose. Many scientists think that we at some stage
lost the ability to make our own, which is why we now
need to take it in large quantities compared to other
vitamins.

WHAT IT DOES Vitamin C has three major roles:
1. As an antioxidant it protects other vitamins from
   destruction, as well as preventing cellular damage. It
   also detoxifies lead, cadmium, copper, DDT, mercury, and many other environmental toxins.
2. It is essential for making collagen, which is our
   "intercellular glue", vital for healthy arteries, youth-
   ful skin, and strong bones and joints.
3. It strengthens our immune system, protecting us
   from colds and flu. It may also have a protective role
   to play against cancer.

SIGNS OF DEFICIENCY Frequent colds and infections, lack of
energy, allergies, wrinkles, premature aging, bleeding gums,
dental cavities, easy bruising, nosebleeds, slow wound
healing, anemia.[22]

WHERE TO FIND IT Highest sources are berries, tropical
fruits, peppers, and fresh vegetables and fruit. The vitamin C content of the same foods varies considerably.

HOW MUCH DO YOU NEED? This can vary from 1,000mg to
5,000mg and sometimes more under conditions of extreme
stress or exposure to pollutants. One cigarette destroys up
to 40mg of vitamin C.
RDA: 45mg (USA); 30mg (UK & Australia); 60mg (New
Zealand); 120mg (USSR)
Optimum range for adults: 1,000mg to 4,000mg

Optimum range for children (aged three to 12): 500 mg to 2,000mg
Single dose toxic level: 10,000mg or more[5]

SUPPLEMENTS Supplements can use ascorbic acid, sodium ascorbate, calcium ascorbate, and ascorbyl palmitate. Sodium ascorbate is best avoided. Ascorbic acid is best when provided with an alkaline filler such as calcium phosphate. Sometimes slight diarrhea can occur with an excess supplementation of vitamin C; however, constipation has also been recorded as a side effect of supplementation.[23]

FRIENDS Bioflavanoids contribute to some of the beneficial effects of vitamin C.

ENEMIES Lead, copper, mercury, aluminium, cadmium, carbon dioxide, rancid oils, smoking, barbecued food, pesticides, DDT, and many other pollutants.

Bioflavanoids
The bioflavanoids consist of a group of substances including rutin, hesperidin, citrin, flavones, and flavonals. They are found together with vitamin C in nature and there therefore sometimes called the C Complex.

WHAT THEY DO Their only known role is that of strengthening the tiny bood vessels, therefore they are particularly important for those with circulatory conditions.

SIGNS OF DEFICIENCY Hemorrhages under the skin, easy bruising.[24]

WHERE TO FIND THEM Rutin is highest in buckwheat, and the others are highest in citrus fruit and other rich vitamin C sources.

HOW MUCH DO YOU NEED? People with poor circulation may need more.
RDA: none established
Optimum range for adults and children: 25mg to 100mg
Toxic level: not known

SUPPLEMENTS The addition of at least 25mg of citrus bioflavanoids to a vitamin C supplement is a sensible precaution against deficiency.

FRIENDS Vitamin C.

ENEMIES All vitamin C antagonists.

Vitamin D

Vitamin D, known as ergocalciferol or cholecalciferol, is made in the skin under conditions of exposure to sunlight. Its production is particularly high in the summer and autumn, presumably in preparation for the winter months. Inhabitants of countries like Britain, which does not have very high levels of sunlight, must obtain a significant amount of vitamin D from their food. Vitamin D is measured in IU or mcg. 40mcg = 1 IU of vitamin D.

WHAT IT DOES Vitamin D is essential for the absorption of calcium and phosphorus, both of which are needed for bone formation. It also helps to release calcium from the bones into the blood, ensuring its proper distribution.

SIGNS OF DEFICIENCY Signs of deficiency are related to bone disorders or disorders of the thyroid and parathyroid glands. Possible signs of these are rheumatism, rickets, backache, tooth decay, muscle cramps, pain and stiffness in the joints, loss of energy, difficulty losing weight, chilblains, dry skin, hair loss, coarse hair, and nearsightedness.[25]

WHERE TO FIND IT Best sources are fish, milk, egg yolk, and the livers of animals and fish, although the last-named are also frequently high in undesirable toxic material.

HOW MUCH DO YOU NEED? Children up to seven need at least 400 IU per day because their bones are growing. Since poor calcium utilization is common among the elderly, extra vitamin D is also recommended for them. The amount needed depends on your exposure to sunlight.

RDA: 280 IU (USA)[4] 100 IU (UK); 400 IU (Australia & New Zealand)
Optimum range for adults: 400 IU to 1,000 IU
Optimum range for children (aged three to 12): 200 IU to 500 IU
Single dose toxic level: not known[5]
Continuous dose toxic level (over three months): 100,000 IU

SUPPLEMENTS Vitamin D is usually supplied as ergocalciferol and occasionally in fish liver oils. These forms are fine. Enough is usually present in a vitamin A supplement or in a multivitamin.

FRIENDS Calcium and phosphorus (phosphate) are needed to make use of vitamin D. As for vitamin A, adequate intakes of C and E protect vitamin D.

ENEMIES None. Vitamin D is basically stable.

Vitamin E

Vitamin E's name is tocopherol, derived from the Greek word for childbirth due to its beneficial effects on fertility. However, it has recently been discovered that some of the properties ascribed to this fat-soluable vitamin were in fact the result of octacosanol, another ingredient found in oils containing vitamin E.[26] It comes in many different forms called alpha, beta, gamma, and delta tocopherol. Alpha tocopherol is the most potent; together they are known as the mixed tocopherols. It is measured in IU or mg. 1mg = 1 IU of alpha tocopherol.

WHAT IT DOES Vitamin E is an antioxidant. It protects against cell damage, helps ensure oxygen supply to the cells, and protects vitamins C, A, and D in the body. If also prevents blood from clotting and helps bring oxygen to the capillaries by dilating them. All these effects make it essential for optimum muscle function. It can provide protection against most circulatory problems including thrombosis, arteriosclerosis, phlebitis, and heart attacks or strokes. It also strengthens the immune system and is excellent for healing scars. Perhaps the fact that 35 million Americans now take this vitamin has made a significant contribution to the USA's declining incidence of circulatory disease.

SIGNS OF DEFICIENCY Loss of sex drive, dry skin, excess sweating, exhaustion after gentle exercise, easy bruising, infertility, slow wound healing, varicose veins, edema, puffy ankles, some forms of cramp, breathing difficulties. Deficiency can also occur when the liver is damaged, such as in alcoholism, and in those with cystic fibrosis.[27]

WHERE TO FIND IT It is so hard to become totally deficient in vitamin E that early experimenters using rats thought that vitamin E wasn't essential because no symptoms of deficiency ever occurred. However, the rats were obtaining their vitamin E from the straw and wood in their cages! It is found in oils—the best sources being wheatgerm, soya, sunflower, safflower, corn and peanut oil. But watch out: some refiners remove the vitamin E before selling you the oil. Always get unrefined "cold-pressed" oil.

HOW MUCH DO YOU NEED? Individual variation is not well researched. You need more if you exercise frequently and if your exposure to anitoxidants is increased by your living in polluted areas, smoking, or often frying your foods (it also depends on the amount of polyunsaturated fat in your diet). If you are taking the drug Warfarin you should not take high doses of vitamin E as it can cause hemorrhages in these circumstances. Symptoms of deficiency are more common in women than in men.
RDA: 15 IU (USA)[4]; none established (UK, Australia & New Zealand)
Optimum range for adults: 100 IU to 1,000 IU
Optimum range for children (aged three to 12): 50 IU to 500 IU
Continuous dose toxic level (over three months): usually over 2,000 IU[5]

SUPPLEMENTS D-alpha tocopherol is the most potent form of vitamin E, but many manufacturers use Dl-alpha tocopherol which is the synthetic and less potent form. Mixed tocopherols are also used because they are cheaper. If the D-alpha tocopherol is in oil form it is called an acetate; in tablet form it's called a succinate. Both are good. People with high blood pressure, or who have had rheumatic heart disease, should not take more than 100 IU to start with. It can then be increased by 100 IU every other week for those with high blood pressure up to a maximum dosage of 1,000 IU. Reactions to vitamin E rarely occur and are often due to wheat allergy when the acetate comes from wheatgerm oil. In such cases simply switch to soy oil as a source.

FRIENDS Vitamin E is a partner of selenium and vitamin C in its role as an antioxidant.

ENEMIES It is destroyed by cooking, especially frying and, to a lesser exent, by freezing. "Ferric" forms of iron are antagonistic, but "ferrous" forms such as ferrous gluconate, are fine. So iron contained in multivitamins with vitamin E should be in the ferrous form.

Vitamin F

Vitamin F, a term that is going out of fashion, describes essential forms of fats. These include linoleic, linolenic, and arachidonic acid. Two more have recently been added to the list—gamma linolenic acid (GLA) and eicosapentaenoic acid (EPA for short.).

WHAT IT DOES All these fatty acids help make hormonelike substances called prostaglandins. These have different effects, one of which is to regulate blood clotting. They are also used to make the insulating layer around the nerve, called the myelin sheath. It is this that breaks down in multiple sclerosis, causing loss of muscle function.

SIGNS OF DEFICIENCY Poor skin condition, irritability, excessive eating, hormone imbalances such as premenstrual tension, poor blood clotting, and circulatory problems.[28]

WHERE TO FIND IT Linoleic, linolenic, and arachidonic acid are in vegetable oils. GLA is produced from linolenic acid, but some people are not very good at making this conversion and need to take in GLA, the best source being the oil of the evening primrose. EPA is highest in oily fish, so it is time for a herring revival!

HOW MUCH DO YOU NEED? Your needs for these fatty acids depend very much on your ability to convert them into prostaglandins. Since only tiny amounts are needed to make the prostaglandins, no supplements would theoretically be required if our bodies were functioning optimally. Those suffering from cystic fibrosis have extra needs for the essential fatty acids.[29] There is evidence that poor use of essential fatty acids is very common.[30]

RDA: none established

Optimum range for adults: 1 to 4 tablespoons of cold-pressed vegetable oil

Optimum range for children (aged three to 12): ½ to 2 tablespoons of cold-pressed vegetable oil

Toxic level: none known

SUPPLEMENTS Supplements of linolenic or linoleic acid are not necessary since vegetable oils are an easier and cheaper source. In some conditions GLA should be supplemented as evening primrose oil, and EPA derived from fish oil.

FRIENDS Antioxidants like vitamins E and C are needed to protect these oils. All polyunsaturated oils (vegetable oils including vitamin F) are easily oxidized and more vitamin E should be taken to protect these. The ideal intake of fat should be below 30 percent of all your dietary calories, with no more than two-thirds of this being saturated in one-third unsaturated.[31]

ENEMIES Again, frying, cooking, and most food-processing are highly destructive of vitamin F.

Vitamin K

Vitamin K refers to a group of fat-soluble chemicals called quinones which can either be made in the intestine or supplied from the diet.

WHAT IT DOES Vitamin K has only one known function: it helps blood to clot.

SIGNS OF DEFICIENCY Diseases in which blood clotting does not occur and bleeding continues, such as hemophilia, are the only situations in which vitamin K deficiency may be involved.[32]

WHERE TO FIND IT It is very high in spinach, cabbage, and cauliflower and is also found in meat and milk.

HOW MUCH DO YOU NEED? Since at least half of one's needs can be supplied through the functioning of the intestines when the right bacteria are present, daily needs are hard to predict. Normally, we get quite enough without any need for supplementation.
RDA: none established

14

A–Z of Vitamins for Common Ailments

While there is no substitute for individual assessment of
nutrient needs, the following nutritional advice is helpful
for those suffering from particular ailments. Many of the
conditions are quite serious and you would be wise to
follow these programs under the supervision of your doctor or nutrition consultant. The supplements recommended
are for adults and are based on the formulas given in
Chapter 12. Since dosage is crucial it is best to get
supplements closest to these formulas.

Acne

Acne is most prevalent among teenage boys and girls and
the hormonal changes that take place at this age are
certainly at the root of many skin problems. These changes
cause the sebacious glands to produce too much sebum,
which blocks up the skin pores and makes them more likely
to get infected. Optimum nutrition helps by balancing
hormones as well as reducing the risk of infection. The
most important nutrients are vitamins A, B Complex
(especially B_6), C, and E and zinc. Good diet and cleanli-
ness are essential.

DIET ADVICE Follow the vitality diet and drink plenty of
water. Sulphur-rich foods such as eggs, onions, and garlic
are also helpful. Avoid sugar, cigarettes, fried and high fat
foods.

SUPPLEMENTS
      2 × Multivitamin
      1 × B Complex

2 × Vitamin C 1,000mg
1 × Vitamin B_6 100mg + zinc 10mg
1 × Vitamin E 500 IU (helps heal the skin)

Alcoholism

Alcoholism is particularly high among high histamine people, and may in part be a way of coping with the excess energy the high histamine person produces. B vitamins, especially B_1, B_2, B_3, B_6, are destroyed by alcohol, which primarily affects the liver and nervous system. Vitamins A and C help protect the liver. A very alkaline diet reduces craving for alcohol. Emotional problems almost always underlie alcoholism and these as well as the addiction—which usually also exists for sugar—must be solved.

DIET ADVICE Follow the vitality diet and eat plenty of wholegrains, beans, and lentils. Drink plenty of water. Often, sugar addiction is substituted for alcohol, which is a different form of sugar, so sugar is also best avoided. Eat frequent meals containing some protein foods such as nuts, seeds, fish, chicken, eggs, or milk produce.

SUPPLEMENTS
3 × Multivitamin
1 × Multimineral
3 × Vitamin C 1,000mg
1 × Vitamin B_6 100mg + zinc 10mg
3 × Dolomite (providing 500mg calcium and 250mg magnesium)

Allergies

Allergy is a word that often invokes connotations beyond its original meaning. An allergy is an intolerance to a particular substance. We have an intolerance to coffee, for example, in that large amounts produce symptoms. Some people have more pronounced symptoms even to simple foods like wheat or milk. Since an allergy is like an addiction, it is often the foods one is most "addicted" to that are suspect. If you suspect that you might have allergies but do not know what they are, it is best to see a nutrition consultant or an allergy specialist. Optimum nutrition will greatly reduce or clear up allergic reactions in most cases.

DIET ADVICE Follow the vitality diet, being careful to avoid the substances to which you react. After two months you may be able to reintroduce these every fourth day without having a reaction. Eventually you may be able to tolerate your allergens in small amounts on a daily basis.

SUPPLEMENTS
> 2 × Multivitamin
> 3 × Vitamin C 1,000mg
> 3 × Vitamin B_6 100mg + zinc 10mg
> 3 × Dolomite
> 1 × Manganese 10mg

Anemia

Anemic symptoms include weakness and fatigue and loss of color in the face. You may feel as though there is a heavy weight on your shoulders. Classically this is due to a lack of iron; however, deficiency in B_{12}, folic acid, B_6, and manganese can all bring on these symptoms. It is wise to have a blood iron test. The following program will help make best use of iron supplied in the diet.

DIET ADVICE Follow the vitality diet, eating plenty of beans and lentils as well as eggs, which are high in iron. Taking these with vitamin C rich foods, like citrus fruit or green peppers, dramatically increases iron absorption.

SUPPLEMENTS
> 2 × B Complex
> 1 × Multivitamin
> 1 × Multimineral
> 1 × Vitamin C 1,000mg
> 1 × Manganese 10mg

Arteriosclerosis and Atherosclerosis

Arteriosclerosis means hardening of the arteries; atherosclerosis means narrowing of the arteries due to fatty deposits. Most of us have some degree of both. When the condition becomes more pronounced, blood pressure begins to increase. Optimum nutrition is most useful for preventing heart disease. Vitamins C and E and selenium help prevent the cellular damage that may underlie these problems. Vitamin C is essential for healthy arterial condition and together with vitamin E and the B vitamins helps to keep down cholesterol levels and maintain the right degree of blood clotting.

DIET ADVICE Follow the vitality diet strictly. Avoid sugar, salt, high fat foods, coffee, and excess alcohol. Take plenty of exercise within your capacity and do not smoke.

SUPPLEMENTS
- 1 × Multivitamin
- 1 × B Complex
- 3 × Vitamin C 1,000mg
- 1 × Vitamin E 500 IU (introduce gradually and work up to 1,000 IU)
- 1 × Multimineral
- 1 × Selenium 50mcg
- 1 × Vitamin B_6 100mg + zinc 10mg

Arthritis

There are two major forms of arthritis and many different causes for both. Osteoarthritis, more common in the elderly, describes a condition in which the cartilage in the joints wears away, inducing pain and stiffness mainly in weight-bearing joints. Rheumatoid arthritis affects the whole body, not just certain joints. Once more the cartilage is destroyed and replaced with scar tissue, which can eventually cause the joints to fuse together. Nutritionally speaking, the primary means to avoid these conditions is to provide support for the endocrine glands that are involved in proper utilization of calcium. Vitamins C, B$_3$, B$_5$, B$_6$, and D, calcium and magnesium are particularly important. Also associated with arthritic conditions are excesses or deficiencies of iron and copper and possibly manganese, all of which are involved in cartilage formation.

DIET ADVICE Follow the vitality diet and be sure to avoid adrenal stimulants such as tea, coffee, sugar, refined carbohydrates such as biscuits and cakes, salt, cigarettes, and alcohol—many arthritic sufferers have eaten excesses of these in the past. Overstressed, often self-employed, people are also more likely to get arthritis. Drink plenty of water and herb teas. Also, have a hair mineral analysis to find your copper level. If it is high don't wear a copper bracelet. (See Chapter 8 for how to reduce your level of copper.)

SUPPLEMENTS
> 1 × Multivitamin
> 1 × B Complex
> 1 × Vitamin C 1,000mg
> 2 × Multimineral
> 2 × Vitamin B$_5$ (Pantothenic acid) 250mg

Asthma

Asthma affects the lungs and respiration and is characterized by difficulty in breathing and frequent coughing. Often asthma attacks are brought on by an allergic reaction, stressful event, or changes in environmental conditions like the weather or a smokey atmosphere. Vitamin A helps protect the lining of the lungs, while vitamin C helps to detoxify environmental toxins. However, for some people the cause of this condition may lie in hormonal imbalances.

DIET ADVICE Follow the vitality diet and see a nutrition consultant or an allergy specialist if you suspect that you may have some allergies.

SUPPLEMENTS

$2 \times$ Multivitamin
$2 \times$ Vitamin C 1,000mg
$1 \times$ B Complex
$1 \times$ Multimineral

Bronchitis

Bronchitis is an inflammation of the tissues of the lung. Optimum nutrition can help prevent this condition by strengthening the immune system and helping to maintain healthy lung tissue. Vitamins A, B complex, C, and E, and the minerals selenium and zinc all strengthen the immune system. Vitamins A and C protect lung tissue.

DIET ADVICE Follow the vitality diet and do not smoke. Have a hair mineral analysis and if your levels of lead, cadmium, or other toxic metals are high follow the detoxifying program in Chapter 8. You may also find some relief from following a diet low in mucus-forming foods, such as milk and milk products.

SUPPLEMENTS

$1 \times$ Multivitamin
$3 \times$ Vitamin C 1,000mg
$1 \times$ Vitamin E 500 IU
$1 \times$ B Complex
$1 \times$ Multimineral
$1 \times$ Selenium 50mcg

Colitis

Colitis is a condition in which part of the large intestine is inflamed. It is often stress-induced; however, it can also be due to allergy and suboptimum nutrition.

DIET ADVICE While the vitality diet is good for some, the high fiber content can act as an irritant in this condition. So a diet higher in cooked vegetables and fruit, steamed fish and cooked grains is often preferable.

SUPPLEMENTS
- 1 × Multivitamin
- 1 × B Complex
- 1 × Multimineral
- 1 × Vitamin C 500mg (a low dosage because vitamin C can irritate the bowel)

Constipation

Contrary to popular belief one should empty one's bowels not once but twice a day. A healthy stool should break up easily and be no strain to pass. By these criteria a large majority of people suffer from constipation. A high fiber diet will help, as will a reduction in meat and milk produce. Exercise is also crucial as it strengthens the abdominal muscles (see Chapter 11). Vitamins B_1 and E help to strengthen these muscles, and vitamin C may also loosen the bowels.

DIET ADVICE Follow the vitality diet with particular reference to eating high fiber foods. Drink at least one pint of water a day, preferably between meals. Reduce your consumption of meat and milk produce.

SUPPLEMENTS
- 1 × Multivitamin
- 1 × Multimineral
- 2 × Vitamin C 1,000mg
- 1 × B Complex
- 1 × Vitamin E 500 IU
- 3 to 6 × Glucomannan fiber 500mg (if the condition is severe)

Cystitis

Cystitis is an inflammation and infection of the bladder, causing frequent and painful urination. Vitamins C and A protect us from such infections, and vitamin C can be particularly helpful at clearing it up.

DIET ADVICE Follow the vitality diet and avoid all sugar. Drink plenty of water.

SUPPLEMENTS

> 1 × Vitamin C 1,000mg
> 2 × Vitamin A 7,500 IU
> 1 × Multivitamin
> 1 × Multimineral
> 1 × B Complex

Diabetes and Hypoglycemia

Diabetes is subdivided into child-onset diabetes and adult-onset diabetes, both being conditions of high blood sugar. Hypoglycemia, or low blood sugar, often precedes adult-onset diabetes. Together, the two conditions are diseases of glucose intolerance. Ensuring the proper production of adrenal hormones, insulin, and "glucose tolerance factor" from the liver is fundamental for all forms of glucose intolerance. Particularly important therefore are vitamins C, B_3, B_5, and B_6, zinc and chromium. People with diabetes must always seek medical advice, and discuss any proposed changes in their diet with a doctor.

DIET ADVICE Follow the vitality diet with the following modifications: eat small, frequent meals containing protein or complex carbohydrates (nuts, seeds, wholegrains, fish, chicken, eggs, cheese, beans, lentils); avoid all sugar and forms of concentrated sweetness, such as concentrated fruit juice, and even excesses of fruit or dried fruit. Also avoid adrenal stimulants such as excessive tea, coffee, alcohol, cigarettes, and salt.

SUPPLEMENTS

> 1 × Multivitamin
> 2 × Vitamin C 1,000mg
> 2 × Multimineral
> 1 × Vitamin B_3 100mg + chromium 100mcg
> 1 × B Complex

Diverticulitis

Diverticulitis is a condition of the small and large intestine, in which pockets in the intestinal wall become distended and are then more likely to get infected and inflamed. The condition, probably the result of not enough fiber and exercise, is rarely seen in primitive cultures. A general vitamin program is recommended to support the muscle tone surrounding the intestines and to maintain a strong infection-fighting system. Increased fiber and regular exercise are the key treatments.

DIET ADVICE Follow the vitality diet, with particular reference to the high fiber foods. Also do regular exercise that strengthens the abdominal muscles (see Chapter 11). Swimming is your best stamina-increasing sport.

SUPPLEMENTS

> 1 × Multivitamin
> 1 × B Complex
> 1 × Vitamin E 500 IU
> 1 × Vitamin C 1,000mg
> 1 × Multimineral

Eczema

Eczema is a skin condition in which the skin becomes scaly and itchy; it can crack and be very sore. Other skin conditions such as dermatitis are very similar in nature and probably in cause. The possibility of allergy must be strongly considered. Although the mechanism is unknown, optimum nutrition does usually help this condition. Vitamins A and C strengthen the skin, while vitamin E and zinc improve healing. When there is no open wound, vitamin E oil can help to heal the skin.

DIET ADVICE Follow the vitality diet. Test for likely allergies, including the effects of metals from watches and jewelry.

SUPPLEMENTS

- 1 × Multivitamin
- 1 × Vitamin A 7,500 IU
- 1 × B Complex
- 1 × Vitamin E 500 IU
- 1 × Vitamin B_6 100mg + zinc 10mg
- 2 × Vitamin C 1,000mg

Gallstones

Gallstones are accumulations of calcium or cholesterol in the duct running from the liver to the bladder, which stores bile used for digesting fats. If this duct is blocked, fats cannot be properly absorbed and jaundice occurs. Excesses of dietary calcium or cholesterol are not to blame, but rather how these substances are dealt with in the body. Often, gallstone victims have inherited very narrow gall ducts, increasing their risk of this condition. Lecithin helps to emulsify cholesterol and optimum nutrition in general should help prevent such abnormalities from occurring.

DIET ADVICE Follow the vitality diet, keeping fat intake low and regular. Avoid meals containing large amounts of fats.

SUPPLEMENTS

- 1 × Multivitamin
- 1 × Vitamin C 1,000mg
- 1 × Multimineral
- 1 × B Complex
- 2 tablespoons of lecithin granules (on food)

Gout

Gout is caused by improper metabolism of proteins resulting in uric acid crystals being deposited in fingers, toes, and joints, resulting in inflammation. Diets low in fat and moderate in protein help this condition as does exercise. However, the many nutrients involved in protein metabolism are also an essential part of a nutritional program for preventing gout.

DIET ADVICE Follow the vitality diet, preferably avoiding red meat. Be sure to drink at least 1 pint of water a day.

SUPPLEMENTS

      1 × Multivitamin
      3 × Vitamin C 1,000mg
      1 × B Complex
      1 × Multimineral
      1 × Vitamin B_6 100mg + zinc 10mg
      3 × Dolomite

Hypertension (High Blood Pressure)

Hypertension (high blood pressure) and arteriosclerosis usually go together. However, hypertension can also be caused by severe anxiety or stress, which also cause a restriction of the blood vessels by nervous control. In these situations, relaxation exercises and methods of controlling stress are essential.

See ARTERIOSCLEROSIS for dietary and supplementary advice.

Hyperthyroid and Hypothyroid

The thyroid gland, situated at the base of the throat, controls our rate of metabolism. In hyperthyroidism or overactive thyroid, symptoms such as overactivity, loss of weight, and nervousness are common; in hypothyroidism or underactive thyroid, the symptoms are goiter, lack of energy, and overweight. Hypothyroidism can, uncommonly, be caused by a lack of iodine, and taking iodine in kelp is advised to help the condition. Since the thyroid gland is controlled by the pituitary and adrenal glands, the nutrients involved in hormone production and regulation for all three glands are particularly important. These are vitamins C and B Complex (especially B_3 and B_5), manganese, calcium, and zinc.

DIET ADVICE Avoid all stimulants and follow the vitality diet.

SUPPLEMENTS

1 × Multivitamin
1 × B Complex
1 × Vitamin C 1,000mg
1 × Multimineral
1 × Manganese 10mg

For hypothyroidism only: kelp with iodine

Indigestion

Indigestion can be caused by many different factors including too much hydrochloric acid production in the stomach. A hiatus hernia usually causes heartburn. In most cases, the symptoms of indigestion can be helped by the following principles of optimum nutrition; in some cases, additional enzymes are needed.

DIET ADVICE Follow the vitality diet, having as much alkaline forming foods as possible (see Chapter 10).

SUPPLEMENTS

1 × Multivitamin
1 × Vitamin C 1,000mg
1 × B Complex
1 × Multimineral
3 × Dolomite

If the basic program doesn't produce results: 1 × Digestive enzymes with betaine hydrochloride with each meal.

Infertility

Infertility is more common in women than men, although in 30 percent of couples who have difficulty conceiving, it is due to the man. Vitamins E and B$_6$, and zinc are important for both sexes, and vitamin C is important for men. Also important are octacosanol and essential fatty acids.

DIET ADVICE Follow the vitality diet. Octacosanol and essential fatty acids are found in cold-pressed vegetable oils. Make sure your diet includes a tablespoon of such oil, preferably in a salad dressing. Make sure the oil is fresh and keep it refrigerated.

SUPPLEMENTS
> 1 × Multivitamin
> 1 × Vitamin E 500 IU
> 1 × B Complex
> 2 × Vitamin C 1,000mg
> 2 × Vitamin B_6 100mg + zinc 10mg

Insomnia

For some sufferers the major problem of insomnia is waking up in the middle of the night, for others it's not getting to sleep in the first place. Both can be the result on the nervous system of poor nutrition or too much stress and anxiety. Calcium and magnesium have a tranquilizing effect as does vitamin B_6. Tryptophan, a constituent of protein, has the strongest tranquilizing effect and if taken in doses of 1,000mg to 3,000mg, it is highly effective for insomnia. It takes about an hour to work and remains effective for up to four hours. While tryptophan is nonaddictive and has no known side effects, its regular use is not recommended—it is better to adjust one's life-style so that no tranquilizing agents are needed.

DIET ADVICE Follow the vitality diet, avoiding all stimulants. Do not eat sugar or drink tea or coffee in the evening. Eat seeds, nuts, and vegetables, which are high in calcium and magnesium.

SUPPLEMENTS
> 1 × Multivitamin
> 1 × Vitamin B_6 100mg + zinc 10mg
> 3 × Dolomite
> 1 × Vitamin C 1,000mg
> 1 × B Complex
> 1 × Multimineral
> 2 × L-Tryptophan 500mg (only if absolutely necessary)

Menstrual Problems

Premenstrual problems as well as menopausal problems can be helped by optimum nutrition. Particularly important are vitamin B_6, zinc, magnesium, and essential fatty acids. While the need for these is greater in premenstrual tension before the period is due, it is wise to take the supplements throughout the month.

DIET ADVICE Follow the vitality diet. Ensure that your diet contains one tablespoon of cold-pressed vegetable oil.

SUPPLEMENTS
>   1 × Multivitamin
>   2 × Vitamin B_6 100mg + zinc 10mg
>   1 × Vitamin C 1,000mg
>   1 × B Complex
>   1 × Multimineral
>   (Gamma linolenic acid, optional)

Obesity

Some of the causes and treatments for obesity are discussed in Chapter 7. Nutrients needed to help maintain ideal weight include vitamins B_3, B_6, and C, zinc and chromium. Lecithin is also reputed to help in the breakdown of fats.

DIET ADVICE Follow the vitality diet, choosing the lower calorie foods where possible. Experiment with fasting one day a week, or sticking to fruit only. Make aerobic exercise a regular part of your day (see Chapter 10). Read Chapter 7, "The five-factor diet".

SUPPLEMENTS
>   1 × Multivitamin
>   1 × Vitamin B_6 100mg + zinc 10mg
>   1 × Vitamin B_3 100mg + chromium 100mcg
>   1 × B Complex
>   1 × Multimineral

1 × Vitamin C 1,000mg
3g Glucomannan fiber per day for three months

Psoriasis

Psoriasis is a skin disease similar to eczema and characterized by red, scaly skin. The same nutritional recommendations apply as for eczema, with vitamin A and zinc being particularly important.

Senility

Senility is primarily characterized by a loss of memory. While this may be caused in part by poor circulation, a decrease in the brain chemical acetylcholine is often found. Vitamins B_1 and B_5, as well as choline, are needed to produce acetylcholine so all these are recommended. Many other nutrients are also involved in maintaining optimum mental function. A hair mineral analysis should be carried out to determine if any toxic levels of metals are present, especially aluminium.

DIET ADVICE Follow the vitality diet, and be sure to drink plenty of water.

SUPPLEMENTS
   1 × Multivitamin
   1 × B Complex
   2 × Vitamin B_5 (Pantothenic acid) 250mg
   1 × Vitamin C 1,000mg
   1 × Multimineral
   2 tablespoons of lecithin granules (on food)

Ulcers

Stomach ulcers occur in the stomach, and duodenal ulcers in the duodenum—the first section of the small intestine, which is not so well protected as the rest of the intestines against the acid secretions of the stomach. In prolonged stress the stomach can oversecrete acid so stress can be a cause. Also, diets that are too acid-forming are to be avoided. Vitamin A is the primary nutrient needed to protect the lining of the duodenum. While vitamin C does help those with duodenal ulcers, not more than 500mg should be taken as it can cause irritation. If a burning sensation is experienced after taking vitamin C the dose is too high.

DIET ADVICE Follow the vitality diet, keeping mainly to alkaline forming foods.

SUPPLEMENTS

> 1 × Multivitamin
> 2 × Vitamin A 7,500 IU
> 1 × B Complex
> 1 × Vitamin C 500mg
> 1 × Multimineral

Varicose Veins

Veins carry the blood returning to the heart. A varicose vein is one that has become enlarged and swollen; it usually occurs in the legs where circulation is most difficult. It is unlikely that optimum nutrition can do much for veins that are already varicose; however, adequate amounts of vitamins C and E as well as other nutrients can help to prevent further occurrences. Also, there is some evidence that a high fiber diet can help to prevent varicose veins.

DIET ADVICE Follow the vitality diet. Regular exercise, especially swimming, will improve the circulation. Hot baths, putting one's feet up, and gentle leg massages are all helpful. Vitamin E application is also beneficial.

SUPPLEMENTS

> 1 × Multivitamin
> 1 × Vitamin E 500 IU
> 1 × B Complex
> 1 × Multimineral
> 2 × Vitamin C 1,000mg

Vitamins for First Aid

Although ongoing optimum nutrition will prepare you for accidents and emergencies, there are many situations in which optimum nutrition can provide immediate relief. All doses stated are for adults, and children's needs should be scaled down accordingly. These doses are not intended for continuous use.

Abscess A localized infection. Increase vitamin C intake to 1,000mg five times a day, and vitamin A in 7,500 IU capsules to four capsules once a day for no more than one week. This will helps strengthen your immune system. Vitamin B_6 100mg twice a day helps to localize the infection and acts as a mild analgesic. Take a B Complex if you're on antibiotics.

Allergic Reaction Sudden allergies can occur because of something you have eaten or been exposed to. Take 500mg of Vitamin B_6 or 5,000mg of vitamin C and drink plenty of water.[1] This will help you to return to normal. Dolomite powder (high in calcium and magnesium) helps to stabilize histamine levels.

Burns Burns need to be treated instantly. Never put on plasters until the heat is out of the burn. To heal it take up to 20,000 IU of vitamin A per day and 30mg of zinc for one week or less,[2] depending on the burn. Vitamin E oil can be applied when the burn is not an open wound. Drink plenty of fluids.

Colds or Flu As soon as you feel the first signs of a cold or flu take 1 or 2 1,000mg tablets of vitamin C every hour,[3] but do not exceed 20,000mg a day. As soon as you no longer feel the symptoms, reduce to 1,000mg every other hour. Take 4,000mg daily for the next three days as a cold can be suppressed for this time. If you are able to saturate your bloodstream with vitamin C fast enough for long enough, most colds do not last. If you get abdominal discomfort you are taking too much. Eat little and certainly avoid sugar and alcohol.

Constipation Rare occurrences of constipation are easily solved with 3g of Glucomannan fiber,[4] taken in two doses of 1.5g. Make sure your diet is high in fiber. If you are frequently constipated take 500mg of Glucomannan three times a day. Drink plenty of water.

Cuts and Bruises From a nutritional point of view, these are the same as burns. Scars from cuts heal up spectacularly well when you take 1,000 IU of vitamin E and apply the oil to the injury site (but only when it is not an open wound).

Exhaustion Total exhaustion is a sign for you to take it easy. Take some days off and if you feel like just staying in bed, do so. Take 500mg of vitamin B_5, 500mg of vitamin B_3 (nicotinamide), and 1,000mg of vitamin C three times a day for one day only.

Hangover The symptoms of excess alcohol are half dehydration and half detoxification. So drink masses of liquids and take a B Complex and 2,000mg of vitamin C twice in the day. If you know you're going to be drinking a lot this is best done before your excesses.

Hay Fever See ALLERGIC REACTION.

Headaches These are often due to tension and are a good way to slow you down. Instead of taking aspirin, or migraine drugs which constrict the blood vessels, try taking between 100 and 500mg of vitamin B_3 in the niacin (nicotinic acid) form, which is a vaso-dilator. Start with the smaller dose. This will cause a "blushing" sensation as will as increased heat and can often stop or reduce a migraine in the early stages.

Indigestion Indigestion can occur for a number of reasons but it is often caused by overacidity, especially if you have had a heavy meal. Therefore drink alkaline mineral waters and take 1,000mg of calcium and 500mg of magnesium, best as a dolomite powder or tablets. These will help to reduce the acidity.

Infections Increase vitamin C intake to 1,000mg five times a day, and vitamin A in 7,500 IU capsules to four once a day for no more than one week. This will help strengthen your immune system. 100mg of vitamin B_6 twice a day helps to localize the infection and acts as a mild analgesic. Take a B Complex if you're on antibiotics. Avoid sugar entirely and ensure that your diet is very healthy.

Leg Cramps Cramps are usually due to calcium/magnesium imbalances. Take 1,000mg of calcium and 500mg of magnesium (preferably as dolomite powder). The condition is, very rarely, due to a lack of salt, after a long run in the heat, for example. Except in these circumstances, it is best to avoid added salt and keep fluid intake high.

Migraine See HEADACHES.

Mouth Ulcers These are very often due either to an allergy or to lack of vitamin A. Take up to 20,000 IU of vitamin A a day. If they don't clear in four days you may need more. However, it is best to consult a nutrition consultant about this. Wheat and grain allergies can also result in mouth ulcers.

Overdose Overdoses of a major sort require immediate medical attention. However, an excess of cannabis, amphetamines, cocaine, or LSD seriously depletes B vitamins so these must be restored immediately. For a "bad trip" on LSD or psyllicybin mushrooms take 5,000mg of vitamin C immediately. Any smoking, whether of tobacco or anything else, destroys vitamin C. Take extra 25mg for each cigarette you smoke, with a maximum daily intake of 4,000mg. Much more important is to stop the habit.

Shock Shock, such as in a car accident, causes a considerable release of adrenaline. Make sure you have the time and place to relax and ensure an intake of 3,000mg of vitamin C and two B Complex tablets over the day.

Stings Stings cause a histamine reaction that isolates the poison. Cooling the sting helps to reduce itchiness, as does taking 200mg of vitamin B$_6$.

Sunburn Sunburn is prevented by using a PABA sunscreen—the most effective sunscreen of all. But once you are burnt, follow the advice given for burns. If you have sensitive skin it is wise to ensure a daily intake of 100mg of PABA.

Conclusion

Everyone would agree with the old adage, "prevention is better than cure", but only a very small part of health care and health research is truly aimed at prevention. Only five percent of the finance available for health research goes into preventative projects. Often early screening for cancer or heart disease is considered to be preventative, but it isn't true prevention—it doesn't stop the disease from forming in the first place, but merely allows medical action to take place at an earlier stage. Unwittingly, we have become caught up in the technology of "crisis medicine", which, sadly, is falling far short of our original expectations. Something has to change, and I believe that the revolution taking place in nutrition now heralds the birth of the medicine of tomorrow—a medicine based not on interference, but on cooperation with nature.

With so many research projects being published every year in nutrition, even the nutritionists are not finding it easy to keep up with their ever-increasing discoveries! But the next generation of doctors still receive less than twelve hours' nutritional training and it is unlikely that this will improve in the near future. Yet many researchers now believe that as much as 85 percent of all disease is, in part, attributable to less than optimum nutrition.

The message of this book is simple. There is no "luck" involved in health, nor are there miracle doctors or medicines (or nutritionists!) that will transform you overnight. *You* have the capacity for health, vitality, mental alertness, and happiness quite beyond normal expectations. And you can reach this level of optimum health by obeying the natural laws that govern the only thing you were born with—your body. These laws include the food you eat, the water you drink, the air you breathe, and the exercise you take. As your life-style and the world around you change, you too must adapt to meet your needs for optimum nutrition. Perhaps more than ever before, your good health is entirely up to you.

Recommended Reading

For those who want to learn more about nutrition and optimum health, the following books are highly recommended:

Dr. Michael Colgan, *Your Personal Vitamin Profile* (William Morrow & Co.), 1982. A thorough and well-researched introduction to the importance of the personal approach to health and nutrition.

Donald Dickenson, *How to Strengthen Your Immune System* (Arlington Press), 1984. Detailed information on optimum nutrition for the immune system. Vital information for those with immune diseases such as cancer.

Patrick Holford, *The Whole Health Guide to Elemental Health* (Thorsons), 1983. The book about minerals, hair mineral analysis, and your health, covering recent breakthroughs in mineral research.

Patrick Holford, *The Whole Health Manual* (Thorsons), 1983. A clear and concise introduction to the basic principles of nutrition, explaining how your body works, how to balance your diet, and how to use vitamins and minerals.

Dr. John Marks, *A Guide to the Vitamins* (Medical and Technical Press), 1975. A detailed biochemical handbook for the major vitamins, but rather technical for the uninitiated.

Dr. Len Mervyn, *Dictionary of Vitamins* (Thorsons), 1984. A truly comprehensive dictionary of vitamins, most useful for immediate reference.

Dr. Richard Passwater, *Supernutrition for Healthy Hearts* (Thorsons), 1977. A thorough investigation of the myth surrounding cholesterol and heart disease. Essential reading for those wanting to prevent circulatory problems with good nutrition.

Dr. Carl Pfeiffer and Barbara Aston, *The Golden Pamphlet* (Brain Bio Center), 1980. A manual for helping those with mental illness from a nutritional perspective.

Dr. Roy Walford, *Maximum Life Span* (Norton), 1983. A journey into the realistic future concerning life span, exploring the role of nutrition in extending healthy life expectancy.

Dr. Roger Williams, *Biochemical Individuality* (Texas University Press), 1956. A thesis on the individuality of man in relation to nutritional requirements.

References

The following references to medical journals, books, and government reports illustrate that the principles of optimum nutrition are based on well-established fact. Every year about 8,000 research papers are published that have relevance to nutrition and health. The 300 or so references quoted here represent only a small proportion, yet they provide a good place to start for the enthusiastic reader. For those unfamiliar with the standard journal abbreviations used throughout, a list of the full titles is given on pp. 208–209.

Chapter 1

1. National Research Council, *Recommended Daily Allowances*, 9th ed., 1980
2. US Department of Commerce, Bureau of the Census, *Statistical Abstracts of the United States*, Washington, D.C., 1980
3. *US DHEW, Healthy United States*, DHEW Publication No. (PHS) 80–1232, Washington, D.C., 1979
4. Agriculture Research Service of the USDA, *Dietary Levels of Households in the United States, Spring 1965*, 12–17, 1968
5. US DHEW, *Ten State Nutrition Survey*, DHEW Publication No. (HSM) 72–8130–8134, Health Services and Mental Health Administration Center for Disease Control, Atlanta, Georgia
6. G. Christakis, "Socio-Economic and Long-Term Effects of Teenage Nutrition: Threat or Threshold to a Healthy Adult Life," Editors' Symposium, New York, New York, 1980
7. MAFF, *Manual of Nutrition* (HMSO, Ref. 342), 1984
8. C. Pfeiffer, *Mental & Elemental Nutrients* (Keats), 1975
9. D. Gerber, MD, *Med. World News*, 13 February 1970
10. B. Spur, *Clin. Phys.*, 1964
11. L. Mervyn, *Dictionary of Vitamins* (Newman Turner), 1984
12. H. Sauberlich, *Am. J. Clin. Nutr.*, 25, 756, 1972
13. R. Hoorn et al., unknown source, 1974
14. A. Morgan, *Int. J. Vit. Nutr. Res.*, 45, 448–62, 1975
15. Ibid., 43, 461–71, 1973
16. NACNE Report (Health Education Council), 1983

17. F. Shorland, *Nutr. & Health*, 2, 2, 105–9, 1983
18. M. Colgan, *Your Personal Vitamin Profile* (Blond & Briggs), 1983
19. *American Medical Association Council on Foods and Nutrition Nutrients in Processed Foods* (Publishing Sciences Group), 1974
20. B. Watt and A. Merill, *Composition of Foods* (US Department of Agriculture), 1963
21. L. Mervyn, unpublished paper
22. J. Spring, *Brit. J. Nutr.*, 41, 487–93, 1979
23. Editorial, "Neural Tube Defects", *Lancet*, 1982
24. P. Passwater, *Selenium as Food and Medicine* (Pivot), 180
25. D. Davis, *J. App. Nutr.*, 35, 17–29, 1983
26. R. Walford, Maximum Life Span (Norton), 1983

Chapter 2

1. M. Golub et al., *Am. J. Clin. Nutr.*, 39, 265–80, 1984
2. R. Williams, *Biochemical Individuality* (Texas University Press), 1956
3. H. Popper and F. Steigmann, *J. Am. Med. Assoc.*, 123, 1108–14, 1943
4. C. Wilson, *Nutr. & Health*, 2, 3–4, 1983
5. M. Colgan, *Your Personal Vitamin Profile* (Blond & Briggs), 1983
6. M. Brush, *Nutr. & Health*, 2, 203–9, 1983
7. G. Kerr, *Current Med. Res. & Opinion.*, 4, 29–43, 1977
8. G. Schrauzer, *Bioinorganic Chem.*, 2, 4, 1959
9. H. Stanstead, *Nutrient Interactions with Toxic Elements* (Wiley), 1977
10. B. Aston, *J. Ortho. Psych.*, 9, 4, 237–49, 1980
11. L. Mervyn, Lecture on minerals at Institute for Optimum Nutrition
12. H. Selye, *The Stress of Life* (McGraw-Hill), 1976
13. A. Morita, *J. Nutr.*, 112, 4, 789, 1982
14. D. Dobmeyer, *N. Engl. J. Med.*, 308, 14, 814–16, 1983; T. Grayboys, *N. Engl. J. Med.*, 308, 14, 835–37, 1983; B. Victor, *J. Clin. Psych.*, 42, 5, 185–88, 1981; P. Disler, *Gut*, 16, 193–200, 1975
15. H. Schroeder, *Circ.*, 35, 570, 1967; also *Am. J. Clin. Nutr.*, 21, 230–44, 1968
16. H. Schroeder, *The Trace Elements and Man* (Devin-Adair), 1973
17. C. Pfeiffer, *Mental and Elemental Nutrients* (Keats), 1975
18. P. Webster, *Lancet*, 1, 578, 1978
19. *Sunday Times* 2 October 1983, p. 13
20. P. Holford, *The Whole Health Guide to Elemental Health* (Thorsons), 1983; G. Gordon, *Osteopathic Annals*, 1983

Chapter 3

1. R. Harrell, *Proc. Nat. Acad. Sci. USA*, 78, 1, 574–78, 1981
2. A. Schauss, Tapes from McCarrison Society Conference 1983
3. A. Kubula, *J. Gen. Psych.*, 96, 343–52, 1960
4. B. Rimland, *Am. J. Psych*, 135, 4, 472–75, 1978

5. A. Schauss, *J. App. Nutr.*, 35, 1, 1983
6. M. Colgan, Tapes from McCarrison Society Conference 1983
7. H. Needleman, *N. Engl. J. Med.*, 300, 689–95, 1979; Winneke, article in *Lead versus Health*, ed. Rutter (Wiley), 1983; R. Lansdown, ibid.
8. R. Walford, *Maximum Life Span* (Norton), 1983
9. C. Pfeiffer, *Mental and Elemental Nutrients* p. 188 (Keats), 1975
10. J. McGaugh, *Animal Memory* (National Academy Press), 1982; K. Davis, *Science*, 201, 272, 1978; N. Sitaram, *Science*, 201, 274, 1978
11. A. Sohler, *J. Ortho. Psych.*, 10, 1, 54–60, 1981; also J. Hopkins Tanne, *Amer. Health*, 2, 5, 48, 1983
12. A. Schauss, Tapes from McCarrison Society Conference 1983
13. Figures from Steven Schoenthaler, Ph.D., California State University
14. E. Silbergeld, article in *Lead versus Health*
15. H. Osmond, *J. Neuropsych.*, 2, 287–91, 1961; A. Hoffer, *Dis. Nerv. Sys.*, 24, 273–85, 1963
16. C. Pfeiffer, *J. App. Nutr.*, 27, 2, 1975; also *Rev. Can. Biol.*, 31, 73–76, 1972
17. A. Sohler, *J. Ortho. Psych.*, 9, 1, 6–10, 1980

Chapter 4

1. R. Parr, *Phys. Sportsmed.*, 12, 3, 127, 1984
2. T. Bunch, *Mayo Clin. Proc.*, 55, 113, 1980; C. Zauner, *Swimming Technique*, 10, 61, 1973; T. Cureton, *The Physiological Effects of Wheat Germ Oil on Humans in Exercise* (C. Thomas), 1972
3. P. Holford, *Racing Cyclist Study* (ION), 1982
4. M. Colgan, *Your Personal Vitamin Profile* (Blond & Briggs), 1983
5. Ibid.
6. R. Reid, *Lancet*, 786, 1 October 1982; G. Lunt, *New Scientist*, 475, 17 August 1978
7. J. Bland, tape-recording of symposium on nutrition, 1984
8. M. Colgan, Mental and Elemental Conference, 1984
9. R. Passwater, *Supernutrition for Healthy Hearts* p. 38 (Thorsons), 1977
10. Editorial, *Nature*, 307, 199, 1984; E. Gruberg, *Beyond Cholesterol* (MIT reprint), n.d.
11. R. Passwater, *Supernutrition for Healthy Hearts*
12. W. Haskell, *N. Engl. J. Med.*, 310, 13, 805–10, 1984
13. I. Rouse, *Lancet*, 1, 5–9, 1983
14. H. Preuss, *Life Sciences*, 30, 879–86, 1982; J. Yudkin, *Nature*, 239, 197–99, September 1972
15. G. McGregor, *Lancet*, 2, 568–70, 1983
16. C. Spittle, *Lancet*, 2, 1278, 1971
17. M. Steiner, *J. Clin. Invest.*, 57, 732, 1976
18. J. Belizan, *J. Am. Med. Assoc.*, 249, 9, 1161–65, 1983
19. T. Dyckner, *Brit. Med. J.*, 286, 1847–49, 1983
20. G. McGregor, *Lancet*, 2, 568–70, 1982

Chapter 5

1. R. Walford, *Maximum Life Span* (Norton), 1983
2. P. Wood, *Lipids*, 14, 417, 1979
3. H. Preuss, *Life Sciences*, 30, 879–86, 1982
4. P. Puska, *Lancet*, 1, 1–5, 1983
5. D. Burkitt and H. Trowell, *Refined Carbohydrate Food and Disease* (Academic Press), 1975
6. E. Kershbaum, *J. Am. Med. Assoc.*, 1, 32, 1964
7. *The Complete Book of Vitamins* pp. 308–13, 444–58 (Rodale Press), 1977
8. F. Sunderman, *Cancer Research* 34, 92–95, 1974; ibid., 36, 1790–1800, 1976
9. E. Braverman, *J. Ortho. Psych.*, 11, 1, 1982
10. S. Omaye, *J. Nutr.*, 747–53, 1974; P. Smith, *Nature*, 247, 1982 and 392–93, 1974; A. Tappel, *Am. J. Clin. Nutr.*, 27, 960–65, 1974
11. R. Shamberger, *J. Nat. Can. Inst.*, 44, 4, 931–36, 1970 and 50, 4, 863–70, 1973; G. Schrauzer, *Ann. Clin. Lab. Sci.*, 4, 6, 441–47, 1974; W. Willett, *Lancet*, 8342, 130–34, 1983
12. R. Shamberger, *Crit. Rev. Clin. Lab. Sci.*, 211–21, June 1971; Cowgill, *Bio. Trace Elem. Res.*, 5, 345, 1983
13. D. Dickenson, *How to Fortify Your Immune System* (Arlington), 1984
14. R. Hodges, *Am. J. Clin. Nutr.*, 11, 180–86, 187–99, 1962
15. R. Gross, *Am. J. Clin. Nutr.*, 60, 188–302, 1980
16. L. Pauling, *Vitamin C, The Common Cold and 'Flu* (Berkley), 1970
17. W. Prinz, *Int. J. Vit. Nutr. Res.*, 47, 248–57, 1977
18. R. Fraser, *Am. J. Clin. Nutr.*, 33, 838–47, 1978
19. R. Ellis, *J. Am. Vet. Med. Assoc.*, 168, 231–32, 1976
20. G. Taylor, *Nutr. & Health*, 2, 1, 47–50, 1983
21. "Gastric Cancer", *Brit. Med. J.*, 1, 684–85, 1982
22. A. Evans, *Lancet*, 2, 1183, 1981
23. L. Hayflick, *Handbook of the Biology of Ageing* p. 159 (Van Nostrand Reinhold), 1977
24. R. Hart, *Proc. Nat. Acad. Sci. USA*, 71, 2169, 1974
25. See reference 1
26. M. Ross, *J. Nutr.*, 75, 197, 1961; R. Walford, *Science*, 215, 1415–18, 1982
27. R. Hartung, *N. Engl. J. Med.*, 3102, 357, 1980
28. S. Calstrom, *Lancet*, 1, 331, 1964; D. Streja, *J. Am. Med. Assoc.*, 242, 2190, 1979
29. See reference 1

Chapter 6

1. P. Walsh, *N. Engl. J. Med.*, 300, 5, 253, 1979
2. R. Pepperell, *Med. J. Aus.*, 2, 774–78, 1977
3. E. Gonzales, *J. Am. Med. Assoc.*, 249, 2747, 1983

4. R. Passwater, Chapter 68 in *The Complete Book of Vitamins* (Rodale Press), 1977
5. C. Pfeiffer, *Mental and Elemental Nutrients* (Keats), 1975
6. J. Spring, *Brit. J. Nutr.*, 41, 487, 1979
7. M. Baumblatt, *Lancet*, 1, 832–33, 1970
8. A. Shojanaia, *Am. J. Obstet. Gynaecol.*, 11, 194–96, 1971
9. M. Briggs, *Lancet*, 2, 1037, 1972
10. J. Halstead, *Lancet*, 2, 278–79, 1968
11. E. Grant, *Nutr. & Health*, 2, 1, 33, 1983
12. *Office of Population, Census and Surveys, London School of Tropical Medicine 1982 Studies in Infant Deaths* (HMSO)
13. A. Treloar, *Int. J. Fert.*, 12, 77–126, 1970
14. US FDA leaflet on contraception, 1978
15. C. Pfeiffer, *The Golden Pamphlet* (Brain Bio Center), 1980
16. D. Bryce-Smith, *Lancet*, 1159, 28 May 1977; also unpublished research
17. M. Golub, *Am. J. Clin. Nutr.*, 39, 265–80, 1984
18. C. Pfeiffer, *Int. J. Environ. Stud.*, 17, 43–56, 1981
19. K. Lawrence, *Nutr. & Health*, 2, 3/4, 181, 1983
20. L. Hurley, *Nutr. Today*, 3, 2, 1968; D. Caldwell, *Nutr. Rep. Int.*, 7, 5, 309–19, 1973; J. Apgar, *J. Nutr.*, 103, 1973; S. Davies, *Yearbook of Nutritional Medicine* (Keats), 1984
21. K. Krishnamachari, *Am. J. Clin. Nutr.*, 28, 182–86, 1975
22. T. Turner, *Lancet*, 283–94, 1977
23. E. Silbergeld, article in *Lead versus Health* ed. Rutter, pp. 217–28 (Wiley), 1983
24. See reference 19
25. D. Miller, *Epidemiology of Diseases* (Blackwell Scientific), 1982
26. See reference 22
27. K. Lawrence, article in *Prevention of Spina Bifida and other Neural Tube Defects* ed. Dobbing, pp. 85–125 (Academic Press), 1983; R. Smithells, *Lancet*, 1, 1027–31, 1983
28. W. Doyle, *Nutr. & Health*, 1, 3/4, 209–12, 1983
29. G. Kerr, *Current Med. Res. Opinion*, 4, 4, 29–34, 1977
30. M. Brush, *Nutr. & Health*, 2, 3/4, 1983
31. P. Holford, *Testing the Effects of Nutritional Supplements on PMS* (ION), 1983

Chapter 7

1. J. Durnin, *Brit. J. Nutr.*, 32, 169, 1974
2. M. Apfelbaum, "Influence of Level of Energy Intakes on Energy Expenditure in Man" in *Obesity in Perspective* ed. Bray (DHEW, Washington), 1973
3. D. Burkitt, *Refined Carbohydrate Foods and Diseases* (Academic Press), 1975
4. D. Jenkins, *Lancet*, 2, 1287–90, 1979

5. N. Painter, *Gut*, 5, 201–13, 1964; A. Brodribb, *Lancet*, 1, 664–66, 1977
6. T. Cleave, *Brit. Med. J.*, 1, 416, 1941
7. J. Stein, unpublished study at University of California at Davis, Cal., 1981
8. Walsh, unpublished study at GNC Research Center, Fargo, N. Dakota, 1982; also H. Kissileff, *Am. J. Phys.*, 238, 14–22, 1980
9. M. Matsuura, *Jap. Diab. Assoc.*, 23, 3, 209–17, 1980
10. *Lancet*, 1, 8123, 1979; K. Ashida, *J. Nutr.*, 1969; K. Doi, *DIAEAZ*, Conference Report, 29, 2, 1A–143A, 1980; S. Kiriyama, *Nutr. Rep. Int.*, 6, 4, 231–36, 1972; K. Tsuji, *Jap. J. Nutr.*, 33, 2, 51–58, 1975; also *Jap. J. Nutr.*, 26, 3, 1968; 27, 8, 1974; 31, 4, 1973
11. US patent application no. 3973, 008
12. P. Holford, *Glucomannan—Does It Really Work?* (ION), 1983
13. H. F. Harlow, *Sci. Amer.*, 200, 68–74, 1959; *Sci.*, 130, 421–32, 1959
14. M. Roberts, *Biology—A Functional Approach* p. 323 (Nelson), 1971

Chapter 8

1. C. Paterson, *Lead versus Health* p. 21 (Wiley), 1983
2. H. Schroeder, *The Trace Elements and Man* (Devin-Adair), 1973
3. *Lead and Health*, DHSS Working Party Report (HMSO), 1980
4. H. Needleman, *N. Engl. J. Med.*, 300, 689, 1979; also Chapter 12 in *Lead versus Health*
5. R. Lansdown and W. Yule, Chapter 14 in *Lead versus Health*
6. Winneke, Chapter 13 in *Lead versus Health*
7. *Occupational Exposure to Lead—The Final Standard*, The Federal Register, 14 Nov. 1978
8. Environmental Protection Agency Cost Benefit Analysis, 9 April 1984
9. J. Annest, *Lead versus Health* p. 53
10. J. Tjell, *Nature*, 280, August 1979
11. J. Barton, *J. Lab. Clin. Med.*, 91, 3, 366–76, 1978
12. M. Moore, *Proc. Nutr. Soc.*, 38, 243, 1979; also *Nutrient Interactions with Toxic Elements* ed. H. Sanstead (Wiley), 1977
13. R. Papaionnou, *J. Ortho. Psych.*, 7, 2, 94–106, 1978; Goyer, *Life Science*, 24, 433–38, 1979
14. C. Pfeiffer, *Journal of Orthomolecular Psychiatry*, 7, 2, 1978 and *Biological Psychiatry*, 17, 4, 1982
15. *Diet and Lead* (Campaign Against Lead in Petrol)
16. L. Florian, *J. Nutr.*, 106, 689–96, 1976; M. Conrad, *Gastroent.*, 74, 731, 1978; see also references 11 and 14
17. See reference 14
18. M. Colgan, Tapes from McCarrison Society Conference 1983

Chapter 10

1. J. Le Magnan, *Hunger* p. 89, ed. Novin, Bray and Wyrwidea (Raven Press, N.Y.), 1976

2. NACNE Report (Health Education Council), 1983
3. L. Mervyn, Lecture at Institute for Optimum Nutrition, 1983

Chapter 11

1. Astrand and Rodahl, *Textbook of Work Physiology* pp. 418–20 (McGraw-Hill), 1970
2. R. Passwater, *Supernutrition for Healthy Hearts* p. 225 (Thorsons), 1981
3. Astrand and Rodahl, *Textbook of Work Physiology* p. 602; H. Taylor, *American Journal of Public Health*, 1962
4. Astrand and Rodahl, *Textbook of Work Physiology* pp. 475–77
5. R. Wood, *Medicine and Science in Sport*, 32, 1981
6. Thaddeus Kostrubala, *The Joy of Running* (Lippincott), 1976
7. K. Cooper, *Aerobics* pp. 13, 107 (Bantam Books), 1968
8. W. Bennett and J. Gurim, *The Dieter's Dilemma* (New York Basic Books), 1983; K. Cooper, *Aerobics*
9. K. Cooper, *Aerobics*
10. M. Roberts, *Biology—A Functional Approach* p. 323 (Nelson), 1973

Chapter 12

1. L. Pauling, *Vitamin C and the Common Cold* p. 27 (Berkley), 1981
2. J. Kinderlehrer, *Natural versus Synthetic* (reprinted in *Prevention* magazine), n.d.
3. M. Colgan, *Your Personal Vitamin Profile* p. 140 (Blond & Briggs), 1983
4. L. Mervyn, unpublished paper on mineral chelation
5. C. Pfeiffer, *The Golden Pamphlet* (Brain Bio Center), 1980
6. P. Holford, *The Whole Health Guide to Elemental Health* p. 29 (Thorsons), 1983
7. H. Schaunburg, *N. Engl. J. Med.*, 309, 445, 1983
8. *Times* Science Report on Vitamin B_6, 1984
9. T. Moore, *Vitamin A* p. 453 (Elsevier), 1959
10. J. Marks, *Vitam. Horm.*, 32, 131–54, 1974; W. Korner, *Int. J. Vit. Nutr. Res.*, 45, 363–72, 1975
11. Adverse Drug Reaction Bulletin no. 82, 1980
12. L. Mervyn, *Dictionary of Vitamins* (Newman Turner), 1984
13. R. Peterman, *J. Am. Med. Assoc.*, December 1962
14. See reference 11
15. M. Briggs, *N. Engl. J. Med.*, 290–80, 1974
16. S. Ayres, *N. Engl. J. Med.*, 290, 580, 1974
17. J. Marks, *A Guide to the Vitamins* (MTP), 1975
18. See reference 17
19. L. Mosher, *Am. J. Psych.*, 126, 1290–96, 1970
20. S. Winter, *N. Engl. J. Med.*, 289, 1180–82, 1973
21. J. Moran, *Am. J. Dis. Child.*, 133, 308–14, 1979
22. See reference 8
23. M. Colgan, *Your Personal Vitamin Profile*
24. F. Klenner, *J. App. Nutr.*, 23, 61, 1971

Chapter 13

1. J. Marks, *A Guide to the Vitamins* (MTP), 1975
2. *AMA Drug Evaluations* (American Medical Association Department of Drugs), 1980
3. Editorial in *Phar. Journ.*, 3 December 1983
4. L. Mervyn, *The Dictionary of Vitamins* p. 172 (Newman Turner), 1984
5. See references 10 and 11 in Chapter 12
6. See reference 12 in Chapter 12
7. W. Cassidy, *Zinc and Copper in Clinical Medicine* ed. Hambidge, p. 59 (Medical and Scientific Books), 1978
8. See note*
9. M. Schneider, *Alcohol and Nutrition* (University of California reprint), n.d.
10–13. See note*
14. E. Gruberg, *Beyond Cholesterol* (MIT reprint), n.d.
15. H. Schaunburg. *N. Engl. J. Med.*, 309, 445, 1983
16. L. Mervyn, *The Dictionary of Vitamins* pp. 25–26
17. C. Pfeiffer, *Mental and Elemental Nutrients* p. 169 (Keats), 1975
18. See note*
19. J. Onjour, *Int. J. Vit. Nutr. Res.*, 47, 107, 1977
20. N. Sitaram, *Science*, 201, 274, 1978
21. C. Pfeiffer, *Mental and Elemental Nutrients* p. 145 (Keats, 1975
22. See note*
23. C. Wilson, *Nutr. & Health*, 2, 3/4, 217, 1983
24. "Bioflavanoids and Vitamin C", *Bestways Magazine*, July 1981
25. See note*
26. T. Cureton, *The Physiological Effects of Wheat Germ Oil on Humans in Exercise* (C. Thomas), 1972
27. See note*
28. C. Fleming, *Am. J. Clin. Nutr.*, 29, 976–83, 1976; A. Hansen, *J. Nutr.*, 60, 565–76, 1958; M. Brush, *Nutr. & Health*, 2, 3/4, 1983
29. J. Rivers, *Lancet*, 642, 4 October 1975
30. K. Stone, *Lipids*, 14, 174–80, 1979; D. Horrobin, *Clinical Uses of Essential Fatty Acids* pp. 3–36 (Eden Press), 1982
31. NACNE Report (Health Education Council), 1983
32. See note*

*For references marked with an asterisk, the following books and journals provide the necessary information:
J. Marks, *A Guide to the Vitamins* (MTP), 1975
D. McLaren, *Nutrition and its Disorders* (Churchill Livingstone), 1981
L. Mervyn, *The Dictionary of Vitamins* (Newman Turner), 1984
M. Rechcigl Jr., *Nutrition and Food* (CRC Press, Florida), 1983
American Journal of Nutrition, British Journal of Nutrition, International Journal of Vitamin Nutrition Research

Chapter 14

1. W. Philpott and D. Kalita, *Brain Allergies* (Keats), 1982
2. E. Underwood, *Trace Elements in Human Health* (Academic Press), 1977
3. L. Pauling, *Vitamin C and the Common Cold* (Berkley), 1981
4. US Patent Application no. 3,973,008

Abbreviations of Journals

Am. J. Clin. Nutr.	American Journal of Clinical Nutrition
Am. J. Dis. Child.	American Journal of Diseases of Children
Am. J. Obstet. Gynaecol.	American Journal of Obstetrics and Gynaecology
Am. J. Phys.	American Journal of Physiology
Am. J. Psych.	American Journal of Psychiatry
Amer. Health	American Health
Bioinorganic Chem.	Bioinorganic Chemistry
Bio. Trace Elem. Res.	Biological Trace Element Research
Brit. J. Nutr.	British Journal of Nutrition
Brit. Med. J.	British Medical Journal
Circ.	Circulation
Clin. Phys.	Clinical Physiology
Current Med. Res. & Opinion	Current Medical Research and Opinion
Dis. Nerv. Sys.	Diseases of the Nervous System
Gastroent.	Gastroenterology
Human Nutr. Appl. Nutr.	Human Nutrition: Applied Nutrition
Int. J. Environ. Stud.	International Journal of Environmental Studies
Int. J. Fert.	International Journal of Fertility
Int. J. Vit. Nutr. Res.	International Journal of Vitamin Nutritional Research
J. Am. Med. Assoc.	Journal of the American Medical Association
J. Am. Vet. Med. Assoc.	Journal of the American Veterinary Medical Association
J. App. Nutr.	Journal of Applied Nutrition
J. Clin. Invest.	Journal of Clinical Investigation
J. Clin. Psych.	Journal of Clinical Psychiatry
J. Gen. Psych.	Journal of Genetic Psychology
J. Lab. Clin. Med.	Journal of Laboratory and Clinical Medicine
J. Nat. Can. Inst.	Journal of the National Cancer Institute
J. Neuropsych.	Journal of Neuropsychology
J. Nutr.	Journal of Nutrition
J. Ortho. Psych.	Journal of Orthomolecular Psychiatry
Jap. Diab. Assoc.	Japanese Diabetic Association

Jap. J. Nutr.	Japanese Journal of Nutrition
Mayo Clin. Proc.	Mayo Clinic Proceedings
Med. J. Aus.	Medical Journal of Australia
Med. World News	Medical World News
N. Engl. J. Med.	New England Journal of Medicine
Nutr. & Health	Nutrition and Health
Nutr. Rep. Int.	Nutrition Reports International
Nutro. Today	Nutrition Today
Phar. Journ.	Pharmaceutical Journal
Phys. Sportsmed.	Physiological Sportsmedicine
Proc. Nat. Acad. Sci. USA	Proceedings of the National Academy of Science of the USA
Proc. Nutr. Soc.	Proceedings of the Nutrition Society
Rev. Can. Biol.	Reviews of Canadian Biology
Sci.	Science
Sci. Amer.	Scientific American
Vitam. Horm.	Vitamins and Hormones

Index

ABOUT THE AUTHOR

PATRICK HOLFORD is the author of *The Whole Health Manual* and *The Whole Health Guide to Elemental Health* and regularly writes for many popular magazines. He also teaches and lectures on nutrition and is the founding director of the Institute for Optimum Nutrition in London, an independent center for the research and practice of nutrition.

BANTAM
SHOP-AT-HOME
C·A·T·A·L·O·G

Special Offer
Buy a Bantam Book
for only 50¢.